OVERTHINKING EVERYTHING
ABOUT SOCIAL MEDIA

INFLUENCE

By Josh Brandon

First published by Josh Brandon Media, 2023

INFLUENCE text copyright © 2023 by Josh Brandon

ISBN: 979-8988477877

Book written and designed by Josh Brandon

ACKNOWLEDGEMENTS

This book is for the dreamers and the workers. Those who want more from themselves and more for themselves. More importantly, this book is for those who want all that more for the benefit of others than themselves. This book is for the person who wants to become a personality and the personality who wants to become a phenomenon.

This book is for the people who want to leave a lasting impression, influence others in a positive and meaningful way, and establish a legacy that will last beyond a viral video. No one can teach you how to "go viral". Be suspicious if anyone tries to tell you otherwise. What this book will do is put you in the right position to create a media personality brand out of yourself that will be most effective and fine-tuned to attract a dedicated core audience. There simply are no guarantees in this business, but the information you will get from this book is a great place to start.

We live in a new age where anything is possible! It has never been easier to be in the public eye. The gatekeepers of the media have lost their clutch on the reigns and restrictions that have kept so many voices from having a platform for too long. This book is for those voices, may they be amplified for the greater good. However, with great power...well we know the saying.

DEDICATIONS

This book came about after a TikTok Live with a panel of friends — a community of like-minded souls connected through social media. Friendships forged through the fire of social discourse and the struggles of social media content creation.

The topic shifted to the struggle. The conversation would go well into the wee hours of the morning covering a number of topics related to content creation and social media. One of those friends (whose feature film I was able to audition for, get cast in, and fly from Tennessee to New York City to act in) shifted the authority of the conversation over to me, as I had been helping him with some of what we were discussing.

I had been working on developing **My Podcast Workshop** for some time already and this conversation was research and development as far as I was concerned. And I got to help my friends with valuable information from a perspective I had that others did not — that we, on social media, are broadcasting!

The Live lasted until after 2 AM that morning. I went to my studio and outlined this book. Over the course of the following six days, I would write *INFLUENCE*. Now, I help others - just like you reading this right now – who want to have control of their content by launching their own platform – a podcast.

So, to my friends, followers, and fantastic family on social media, I thank you for inspiring me to speak *my* truth and follow *my* dreams of helping others.

Whatever your content creation journey is, just step out there and speak your truth. Your audience is waiting to find you...

And remember!

Don't *Just* **Create**...

INFLUENCE!

DISCLOSURES

There is no guarantee offered for anything in this workbook or supplemental material. The information presented herein represents the views of the author as of the date of this publication. This book is for informational purposes only. The author reserves the right to alter, update, or reconsider his opinion at any time. The author, nor partners/affiliates, assume any responsibility for any omissions, errors, or inaccuracies. Any reference to any person or business whether living or dead is purely coincidental.

The author is not a licensed or credentialed mental health expert. Any and all advice regarding mental health, therapy, etc. is not professional or medical advice and should not be interpreted as such. The author is not a licensed or credentialed Certified Media Consultant. Any consulting of others, personal or professional, referenced herein is purely on an individual and independent basis.

Contents

6

For more info on:

SUPPLEMENTAL PDF TOOLS AVAILABLE ONLINE

(CHECK THE END OF THE BOOK FOR FULL DOWNLOAD INFO)

INTRODUCTION

There is a responsibility that comes with a platform of mass communication. This book will help you understand that responsibility through the lens of journalism, factual and pragmatic news reporting, broadcast media standards, while more clearly defining how you can fit in to today's media landscape. Not only that, but how you can improve, excel, and sharpen your talents and brand yourself as a Social Media Influencer or Personality. In the off chance you "go viral" or "make it", this book will help ensure you and your content are ready for an audience to take notice.

Thank you for beginning this journey. I believe what I've learned in my three decades of experience in media can help you grow as a talent, content creator, and as a much bigger brand. From print journalism, television news, media program and event hosting, radio programming, broadcasting, talent coaching, and consulting, I have touched many areas of the entertainment industry and being an entertainer. My radio career was spent as an on-air personality and later in life, I took the plunge to invest in myself and follow my dreams of voiceover and acting. While your dreams and goals may differ from my own, I believe mine is a formula for success, both as an example of what to do as much as what not to do.

In this book, you will take the journey from "Who am I" to "What's Next", with ideas, advice, and philosophies that should be beneficial along the way. This book is not designed to be a cheat sheet or even a checklist for you to achieve instant success. This book is, however, designed to answer some questions and provide you with valuable perspective as you embark on your adventure.

This book is broken up into six sections, which will assist you with figuring out who you are and why you want this, how you can do this better and why you need to take it seriously, and how you can take the next steps to be more than you ever thought possible. This book also references additional materials available, that will help further define your "you-ness".

Growing an audience takes time, effort, focus, <u>and</u> strategy. This book will take you down the journey of self-discovery to self-actualization, to the pursuit of a much bigger idea of yourself. You will learn how to assess yourself as a talent and how to relate yourself to an audience. You will learn specific strategies and best practices for creating compelling content that cuts through the clutter. In the end, we are subject to the algorithm and there is only so much we can do about that. However, making sure your content is sharp, authentic, and reflective of your greater mission in life is vital on the off chance you hit that algorithm sweet spot and "go viral". If you do, this book will better prepare you for a larger audience to discover and appreciate your work.

Social media is the mad scientist's hybrid of broadcast investigative journalism, reality television, documentary filmmaking, cable news opinion panels, and radio morning show entertainment. Honestly, there is a lot more we could toss into this metaphorical stew, but for the sake of what you need to know, let's discuss why what you will learn in this book is important.

There are legal, ethical, and societal considerations we should acknowledge before turning on a microphone or camera to communicate with others. While social media isn't regulated by the Federal Communications Commission the way broadcast media is, many of the standards and practices put in place for broadcast media make sense in the social media spaces. The absence of some of these standards creates a muddled and dangerous space of rage farming, misinformation, and bullying.

How the consumer receives a message is different than how we might communicate that message. Our intent and context could be lost in the seconds between us making that point and the audience member tuning in just after that, in time to take whatever you are saying next however they perceive. First impressions are hard to overcome. That is why being deliberate in our thought process in how we formulate ideas and create content around them is key to growing yourself as a branded personality.

Many content creators, podcasters, and modern media personalities create content that is similar to or inspired by content they have seen on other platforms by other creators that appealed to them. Don't reinvent the wheel, as they say. For example, many people host livestreams they treat like a cable news opinion panel. They have a host, sometimes a guest-host or co-host, and they invite people onto the panel to discuss various topics and issues.

Without raining on anyone's popularity parade there are reasons those professionally platformed programs and hosts are as big as they are. Those reasons are preparation, dedication, and upholding some level of standards, whatever those might be. Yes, major media gatekeepers, resources, and money do come into play, but I can't help you with that.

Social media is very much like reality television, too. Many creators don't have a set with a news desk or a backdrop. Most of the time they are in their car, bedroom, living room, just relaxing while chatting with some friends. This gets confusing for the audience, who receives this program (because that's what it is) as a casual chat among people just like them and an informative, sometimes educational, experience.

For years news was buttoned up suits and ties, hair and makeup, lights-camera-action. The shock of skewing the lines of opinion and facts was significant. There was a time the evening news didn't include editorializing, and if it did then it was clearly disclosed.

We are the modern-day media. No disclosures. No distinction between fact and feeling, creative conjecture or the truth and nothing but the truth.

We are entertainment. Journalism. Information. Education. But we are also rapidly replacing media like radio and television. Consumers are turning to social media to not only stay informed, but to occupy their attention. So, as this evolves, don't let it get to your head, but acknowledge the reality of your goals, dreams, and journey while taking charge of your destiny. Set yourself apart from the pack and be prepared to learn some of what I've learned over my years in the entertainment industry, broadcasting and social media, marketing, advertising, and more.

Section 1:

SELF-AWARENESS, SELF-DISCOVERY, AND SELF-ACTUALIZATION

This section will help you define, refine, or redefine yourself as an influencer, personality, and talent. In the social media landscape, it can be difficult to figure out where you fit into it all. In a world where anybody can turn on a camera or microphone and build an audience, how do you capture that lightning in a bottle?

Simple.

Authenticity.

An audience identifies with whom they can relate. There are many other reasons, which have to do with specific niches, talents, content, styles, and more. For this section, we will focus on answering the hard questions like "who are you", "what do you want", "how will you get it", and "who do you want to do it for". Most importantly, this section will ask "WHY do you want this".

At the end of this section, we will have the hardest talk of all – the one we have with ourselves – where we confront the reality of just what kind of journey we are embarking.

IDENTIFYING YOURSELF

"Just be yourself", "You do you, booboo", "To thine own self be true" and every other cliché that comes to mind, the first step is always the hardest. When I consult clients – or talent – who come to me asking how I got into acting, got on television, got into voiceover, built a podcast, brand, and social media following, some are asking out of curiosity. Many are asking because they're afraid of asking the real question they want to ask:

"Josh, how do I do what you have done?"

While I am realistic about the limitations of my accomplishments, to someone who secretly dreams of acting or doing voiceovers, etc., some of what I know might be helpful.

Many are just afraid to ask. Not afraid to ask me, mind you. It is a permission we lack, by society and our environment, support system, or traumatic past. We might not feel like we need permission to pursue our potential, but often that is a major hurdle standing in the way of our efforts. That permission can come in the form of financial investment, supportive reassurance from your close friends and family, or just internally, telling yourself you are allowed to want something.

Once you obtain that much needed permission, you can begin to think about yourself in different ways. For the purposes of this book, I will use the example of a social media personality. To admit to yourself that you would like to have a platform to share your talents, skills, or ideas, and that you would like people to be exposed to and respect those might seem self-important, self-indulgent, or by some misinterpretation of the definition, narcissistic.

Intent means everything.

Being honest with yourself, yet realistic, while still clinging to the hope you need for motivation might sound like an insurmountable challenge. However, it's the first step to self-discovery.

Self-awareness of your abilities, capabilities, and limitations will help you enhance, develop, and overcome, respectively.

So, reader! To quote The Who, "Who ARE You?"

Ooh! Ooh! Ooh! Ooh!

What I am about to say might sound contradictory or hypocritical. The challenge of being a personality is to remain authentic and genuine, yet a caricature of your real self. Genuine authenticity is relatable and something many in your audience will appreciate. Moreover, they will detect the opposite very quickly. As we will discuss soon, your audience's attention span might be miniscule, but that does not mean they will fall for fake.

However, real isn't always interesting, is it?

Go to a theme park and find that skilled artist doodling away with some happy couple. You walk past and see that they have drawn large foreheads, puckery duck lips, larger-than-life eyes, and these goofy expressions. The artist has even changed their clothes!

This is a caricature. While an equally talented artist could sketch what you actually look like, a caricature artist puts boring ol' you through a funhouse mirror reflection. That's far more interesting.

This is not to say you are boring, but I assure you that if you see someone on social media or other media and you think they must be so fascinating and interesting, in most cases (SPOILER!), they're just as boring as we are. What they are good at is not "mugging for the camera" or "faking it". It isn't performative, but it is performance.

"This is me, but more me than I normally might be if you weren't watching me right now."

What you can do to help define your personality so that others will engage with it is to filter yourself through that funhouse mirror of caricature. Look at yourself as a character more than just someone doing their thing.

I had someone tell me once they were just a grandma who made videos people liked watching. When I asked what else set them apart, they struggled to answer. We are not often granted permission, by society, our environment, or our own mental health, to admit to ourselves what it is we truly want. Therefore, we see ourselves as "just _____" and not much else. Some of this is genuine humility and some is societal gaslighting. For everyone who has ever had a dream, there has been an army of doubters there to knock that dreamer back down to reality. The sad fact is most people will never step out on that precipice of popularity for the fear of failure and the resonant ramifications of rejection. Many simply cannot handle what comes with trying to be more than you are. Most get a small taste of it and decide it is not for them. That is ok, too. Being on social media is difficult on many levels, as we will discuss.

That grandma had a story, interests, and personality traits that were the reason people liked watching her videos. She was not "just" a grandma. She was a young-looking, vibrant woman with a larger-than-life personality that drew people in. Sharing her love for her family and frustrations in a funny fashion made her content relatable to a larger base than perhaps if her content was more critical and complaining. While we can all relate to critical and complaining, negativity is off-putting and draws in other negative people seeking validation for their negativity. Especially with her content about family, coming from a more positive place paid off for her. She had to look beyond cat videos and videos about the grandkids to find a much broader groove, and you can too.

Imagine a creator who is a coupon clipper and discount diva! Their niche is making that paycheck stretch. Their target audience comes to them for ideas to feed a family on $25 or less. That may be interesting enough to build a brand by itself. However, the deeper motivation for that creator might be a value that goes beyond budgeting. Discovering that underlying motivation will help solidify your place with your audience and make you a valuable authority in their daily lives, off social media, where their word-of-mouth will bring more consumers to your content!

The following sections can help refine your character and motivation. But, first, you must define who you really are before creating your "character".

The idea that your favorite news anchor would break from delivering the information to share an aside about their pet is not out of the realm of reality. In broadcast news that is referred to as "Happy Talk", among other things. That Happy Talk is the filler at the end of the news broadcast after all the bad news has been delivered where the anchors discuss weekend plans or other small talk designed to not only add some personality to the anchors, but also levity to end the show. There are not many ways news can feel good. However, a little peek into their real lives beyond the teleprompters can end the show on a lighter note while making the audience feel more connected to the hosts – adding positivity and relatability.

Chances are your journey to social media influence is not about becoming a news anchor, but there is an element of journalism, hosting, and entertainment that goes along with it. If you are hosting a program of any sort, you are elevating yourself above the audience. You are the one on camera, talking, commanding the attention. What sets you apart enough to be the person they should spend their time with? What makes you so special? Where is your authority? Why should they watch you over anyone else?

These are valid and important questions to ask yourself as you look at an audience asking them for the most important gift they have to give someone else – their time. Their attention, loyalty, and time are valuable. Often, these are overlooked or taken for granted by even professional media personalities.

There are so many options for an audience's attention. This section, this book, and the tools available can help define you in this space and help you refine your place in the social media clutter.

IDENTIFYING YOUR CHARACTER

Becoming a personality while maintaining authenticity might seem contradictory. It might seem an arduous task of balancing performance with performative. Attempting hilarious can toe the line of coming off histrionic. How do you maintain your genuine self while amplifying the characteristics that will set you apart?

Characteristics! The root word, character, gives us a hint as to what I'm talking about. We have many characteristics about ourselves, our personalities, and our lives – many we never even think about.

How would you describe yourself?

How would others describe you?

What are your three best and worst qualities?

What three interests might someone attribute most to you?

How do those compare with your actual interests?

Think of your favorite television shows that have an ensemble cast. Friends, Seinfeld, The Golden Girls, The Office are all classic examples that have stood the test of time, whether their targeted humor has not as well.

In these programs, consider that each character is one-dimensional. In that, when you think of The Golden Girls, Sofia is the sassy one, Blanche is the sexy one, Rose is the ditzy one, and Dorothy is the bossy one. From there, each woman embodies other traits and characteristics throughout the series, but when breaking down a character analysis, many TV characters are primarily one-dimensional with a few sub-traits that flesh them out a little more. This is not to say that Blanche also can not be ditzy, bossy, or sassy, or that Dorothy must always be the bossy one, but those characters are caricatures of real people's personality traits. And we ALL know people who are like that. We relate to those ladies. That is why the show is a classic.

Now, look at the characters in Seinfeld or Friends. We could do a similar character breakdown for each of these shows. Of the main characters in Friends, for example, Ross, Chandler, Joey, Monica, Phoebe, and Rachel are largely singular one-dimensional personality traits entire characters are built around. In reality, most of us are not as one-dimensional, but thanks to 24/7 pop culture binge-watching always in your face entertainment, we may be heading toward that sooner than we might think.

With Friends, many of us embody the quirkiness and whimsy of Phoebe, but also the no-nonsense-ness of Monica. Or, maybe we are more Monica and wish we could be a little more Phoebe. Most of us know a Joey or two. Ross, the lovesick intellectual or Chandler the wisecracking everyman, are relatable to us because they either are us or we know someone who is. One of our friends, pun intended.

Seinfeld is another good example of character development. I might argue that Jerry, George, Elaine, and Kramer are, in fact, one person. There are aspects of us that are each of those characters, in some part. However, For Entertainment Purposes Only, the writers took these traits and built different, contrasting characters out of them.

Another solid example is The Office. The show crafted characters out of largely singular traits that audiences could relate to. We have all worked for the bad boss. We have all experienced overzealous, nosey, creepy, weird, annoying, motherly, slow, lazy, promiscuous, ambitious, closeted, self-important, naïve, pretentious, or fish-out-of-water coworkers. With Dwight, Angela, Toby, Creed, Kelly, Phyllis, Kevin, Stanley, Meredith, Darryl, Oscar, Ryan, Erin, Andy, or Jim, we were given a glance at a diverse American workplace full of flawed characters who not only were easy to relate to, but easier to identify. In fact, while Toby and Creed could interchange for creepy and weird, or Dwight might be overzealous, pretentious, ambitious, and self-important, some of the traits mentioned identify more with one character primarily, while for others might be considered more sub-traits.

Creating a character of yourself for social media is very similar to character development in a popular hit sitcom. Take yourself through that same one-dimensional lens. What is the singular trait that defines you, as a character? It is harder than it seems. But, if you do not do this for yourself, I assure you that your audience will do it for you. I think you will find that controlling your own narrative will work best in the end. Remember though, as we will discuss later in the book, one-dimensional talent breeds one-dimensional results. Take a note from those classic sitcoms. They have a one-dimensional trait from which they build a character. The character is not one-dimensional, however. One-dimensional traits do not make for interesting characters. Those are simply a foundation on which to build the other identifying sub-traits that will round out that character, making them more relatable to a broader audience, and giving them more opportunities for development and story arcs within the show.

Just as with yourself, find that one primary trait which will be a foundation to which your audience can relate. It should be a likable trait if you want them to like you. Then, isolate your sub-traits in a way that prioritizes those in a hierarchy that is authentic to you.

Remember my warning against letting others define those traits – your character! You do not want to fall into a trap of being something to someone else that does not accurately represent you or your values.

Here's an example from my own life that I believe fits perfectly!

Type-2 Diabetes, high blood pressure, and higher-than-I'd-like cholesterol notwithstanding, I have always loved bacon. At least part of that is because breakfast sausage and I don't get along, digestively speaking. So, I've always gone with bacon as a breakfast protein, and later as a topping on salads, burgers, pizza, and pasta. However, it isn't _that_ much a part of my persona. No more than any other food I enjoy. Between my radio career and acting career, I spent a few years in automotive retail while I rebooted myself and moved back to Tennessee to fight for custody of my daughter. Living closer to my mother than I had in years, I would stay with her sometimes. Mom would get a literal BOX of bacon from the discount grocer, and I would wake up the next morning to the smell of smokey, salty goodness sizzling in the pan. My mother would then pack me up a gallon plastic zip storage bag of bacon and send me off like a child for school. Before long, the crew at the car dealership began to take notice of this slightly overweight, mid-to-late 30's guy coming into work with a bag of bacon. Being the boys' club locker room of testosterone that it was, the jokes did not take long to manifest. Whether I liked it or not, this, eventually, became part of my work character.

It is true that I loved bacon. I snacked on it through the day like jerky, hence the eventual Type-2 Diabetes, high blood pressure, and higher-than-I'd-like cholesterol. It did not matter that the gallon bag would last me a few days, or less if the boys got their hands on it. I was the guy who loved bacon SO much, I carried around a big bag of it. Before long, people were posting bacon memes on my social media. Customers brought me bacon and bacon related items. Friends got me bacon-themed gifts. At one time, I had gotten a jar of bacon jam, a bacon apron, a bacon T-shirt, and a coffee mug that said, "I wish this was bacon".

Friends, I enjoy bacon, but I do not like bacon that much. In fact, all that made me realize I had created this character trait of myself that, while entertaining, was not nearly the most interesting thing about me. Still, to some if you asked them even today, they might say "Oh, yeah! The bacon-in-a-bag guy!".

It does not take much to leave an impression, especially when that impression stands out as unique. After all, who else do you know just has a zip storage bag full of pork products in their desk drawer? This was not necessarily inauthentic, as I truly did enjoy bacon. It was just a caricatured trait that amplified and took off on its own. Sure, I played that up a bit, but eventually, the treat train came to a halt, and I backed off the bacon, thanks, in large part, to the prediabetes diagnosis.

Creating a character out of yourself is not as difficult as it might seem. It goes back to the amusement park example, picturing yourself drawn on that easel with exaggerated features. "Are my teeth really like that?!" No, but filtered through the distorted lens of funhouse mirror, maybe.

When looking at yourself and your physical characteristics, be mindful of your mental health, though. The phenomenon of "if you say it enough times it becomes reality" is very real. **Self-deprecation is you gaslighting yourself to believe the worst about yourself is true.** So, I caution you to be wary of the impact of your words, thoughts, and self-considerations when developing your character or persona.

This is why being "the fat guy" or "the guy with the big bushy beard" may not be the best approaches to take. These are traits that, if you allow them to define your character, when you lose weight or shave, you are left starting from scratch. Plus, when you make fun of yourself, you risk making fun of your audience who also relates to those traits. Body shaming yourself may seem like fair game, after all who are you really hurting but yourself, right? And you know you are kidding, so it's all good, right?

Wrong.

Imagine your audience relates to you because of various reasons and maybe one of those is your body type. When the consumer hears you denigrate yourself, even in humor, you risk their impression being that you think less of them because they are like you and you do not like you, as you are. What are the chances you would like them? Body positivity while maintaining a healthy outlook on physical fitness is optimal. Be realistic, forgiving, and positive – to yourself and others.

Another example that relates from my own personal experience is the body image issue. My father struggled with his weight and that left me with a lot of thoughts and ideas when it comes to my relationship with food, my body, my health, and my self-image. As a comedian, entertainer, and someone who has always had a larger-than-normal personality, my humor's boundaries were not always in line with my own values.

While I had gained some weight during one period of my life, having bacon-bagged myself to nearly 300 pounds, I felt horrible about my image, I felt horrible in general, and I took that out on myself – For Entertainment Purposes Only.

The problem with that was, while I made people laugh with my self-deprecating humor, two other negative side effects manifested from that:

1) My mental health degraded. I began to believe the things I said so often, and my self-worth and self-image deteriorated. This affected my performance at work, my confidence, and my overall attitude.

2) I was not that big. The fact is I have always carried extra weight, mostly in my abdomen. Dad bod. Others might carry theirs all over. For me, waistbands and shirt sizes were the main clothing issues. Others struggle with finding any clothes that fit well because they carry weight in the back, or all over. My humorous comments, directed only at myself, undoubtedly hurt others, too. That was not my intent, nor did I really consider the fact that what I was saying about ME was being received as "if he thinks that about himself and he's much smaller than I am he must think horrible things about me".

Neither of those was my intent. I just wanted to roll with the flow of the jokes others made or cut their jokes off at the pass – beat them to the punchline. If I say I am fat, then it becomes less impactful when someone else says it and I feel safer under the scrutiny of my own self-abuse than I do under the abuse of others.

I did not want to look at someone and ridicule their struggles, I just sought to lighten my own load, so to speak. I was not even trying to BE a character, at least not intentionally. I realize today that is what I was doing because I was trained and conditioned to do that from my radio career. However, others hearing my words about myself reflected to them how I must feel about them and others.

Worse than that, I did not look as heavy as I weighed. It might have been a bit dysmorphic, but I saw myself bigger and unhealthier or out-of-shape than I actually was, at times. Someone else whose body image suffered more than my own would look at me with resentment because there I was complaining about being SO overweight when I was a fraction of their body mass.

This is not to say that physical or other characteristics are off the table for character considerations, it is to say that careful and deliberate scrutiny should be imposed on some characteristics to ensure that we are leaving our audience with an overall positive experience. The idea of creating a character is not to have an all-you-can-laugh buffet of punchlines, but to have those traits be the things the casual consumer can instantly and easily identify with that will make you stand out. More importantly, if one chooses a physical trait to identify themselves, it runs the risk for those in your audience affected by those characteristics, feeling the insecurities that go along with that, seeing someone in a position of influence using or misusing that trait, feeling negatively, whether about you, specifically, or not.

Building character and building A character go hand in hand, sometimes. In this regard, if our character is forged by our failures, then when building a caricature of ourselves, we are misshapen by our mishaps.

What makes you YOU? Are you a parent? What is interesting about your life or experience as a parent? Do you practice a specific trade? What is your expertise? Just like with my grandma and coupon clipper creator examples, dig deeper. Dial that in and then dial that up.

While in most of my content and especially my show, **Overthinking Everything**, I speak a great deal about "cultism" and the unhealthy attachments or inappropriate prioritizations of less important ideas on our hierarchy of values, being aware of that slippery slope is essential. Taking things too far can be funny to an audience. With any "schtick", it can become overplayed, causing audience fatigue. However, these interests can be a goldmine for character creation. It also comes with caveats.

Someone whose entire personality is built around a sports team, band, or brand is not that interesting. Someone who attributes too much of their persona to someone else's success is not special. When you are seeking to stand out in the crowd, you want to be special. There is nothing wrong with wanting to be special. But being the person who loves a thing is not the story. Why do you love the thing you love so much and why is it such a big part of who you are? There is a story. Doing content in your space with the sports team or band paraphernalia behind you is only so interesting to a small number of people. After a while, you become as boring as those trinkets and items are to most of your audience, who might not care as much for those specific things as they care for your unique perspective and ideas.

Now let's discuss the phenomenon of Audience Capture!

Think of it like doing a social media account for silly cat videos and routine around the house content. Then, one day, you get amped up about an issue and post a video ranting about that. That video goes viral; however, it has nothing to do with what you want to do online or what you have done before that viral sensation. When you try and go back to the cat videos, your views drop and you stop growing your audience as fast as you did with the viral video, so you shift your content more toward the nature of that viral video. Now, you're in the cycle of Audience Capture.

The phenomenon of Audience Capture is where one creates content that garners attention. Then, in an effort to ride that wave and convert it into more attention, the creator does more of the thing that got the attention. Before long, the creator finds themselves doing the thing that got the attention, but it may not quite be what they wanted when they started. Then, when they try to go back to, for example, the cat videos, their new audience tunes out. It can seem like they don't want <u>you</u>. They want the you <u>they</u> know.

To avoid the Audience Capture trap, it's important to build your brand on a foundation that makes sense for you and stay true to that. Authenticity is first, and foremost, the most important factor. Your audience will know when you are faking it. That can come off as performative and disingenuous. That is a strong turn-off to many content consumers – especially your loyal followers you hope to convert into fans. Your audience can get fake anywhere. They are turning to you FOR you, so make sure your content and platform is authentic to you. However, you are not so one-dimensional as one of those sitcom characters, are you? How do you branch out beyond Audience Capture while showcasing more than just one side of you?

Creating your character is about evolution. Balancing the phenomenon of Audience Capture and the evolution of shifting gears in your content can be challenging. However, rather than "shifting gears" or changing direction completely, imagine this as pivoting.

Just as in basketball, once you have possession of the ball, you must constantly remain in motion with the ball, dribbling. Once your feet stop moving and you stop dribbling, you can't start dribbling and moving again. That will get a whistle blown with a penalty for travelling. In the realm of social media content creation, this, too, is important and relevant.

Once you "get the ball" on social media, or more aptly put, once you "take off" with momentum, you must stay in fluid motion, dribbling the ball. While there is no referee to call you on your fouls, unless we want to consider getting "cancelled", the data will show you often that consistency is king. In basketball, the trick to avoiding a travelling violation is pivoting. Imagine you have a nail through one of your feet. That foot is planted on the court, and you cannot lift it off. You can spin any which direction on that planted foot, looking for any open teammate to pass the ball, but you may not lift that foot off the court. In this example, your social media momentum is the ball and the other interests or aspects of your personality, or character, are the open teammates. You want to pass the momentum off to another side of you without altogether starting over or causing your audience to "blow the whistle", so to speak. That can be confusing for your audience, who has come to know you for this path you're currently on and can run the risk of them tuning out as much as it can them seeing another side of you. In this case, your planted foot, with the imaginary nail through it, is the foundation of your social media persona, your character. The caricature of yourself.

Make sure, whatever you do, one foot is planted firmly in the character or content niche you want to be in and be known for. That foot does not move. Stay true to that because that will be your most significant path to increased growth. However, diversity in talent, perspective, and persona is quite beneficial in the long term. Establish possession of the momentum ball, plant your foot firmly, and pass the ball to the open aspect of your personality. Sooner or later, you might get an open shot.

Deciding who you are, defining who you want to be on the social media space, and building a solid foundation from which to create content can help avoid the traps and pitfalls so many people make, who come into the journey unprepared, undefined, and indecisive on who they are and what they are about. In everything, authenticity is the single factor that can make or break a creator. If what you are saying is real to you, the audience will relate to that. Stand out from the crowd by building a character – a persona – that audiences will find interesting enough to watch repeatedly. Work to ensure that is always grounded, real, and earnest in intent or you risk becoming more than the caricature of yourself. Trying too hard can come off cartoonish, which is only entertaining for a short while before the average consumer will see through the façade and interpret it as a put-on, For Entertainment Purposes Only.

It is a fascinating time to be alive. Literally anyone can become a social media influencer and personality. Whether your audience is 5 or 5 million, the idea of sharing your ideas, views, and talents with the masses has never been more realistic! The goal here is to come off as interesting as a celebrity without seeming like you are trying to be a celebrity when you are not.

IDENTIFYING YOUR MISSION

When one steps up on the soapbox, so to speak, there is a responsibility to affect some sort of change. This is not to say that everything you do as a content creator should be heavy, deep, and important to the greater good. That is always a good philosophy to embody. However, even if you choose to do cat videos, the underlying mission is a love for animals. That could very well lead into the well-known Bob Barker closing lines of the classic Price is Right, "Remember to control the pet population and have your pets spayed and neutered". Bob was an animal lover and used his platform to address the concerns for the feral pet animal issue.

What would you do if you had that platform and could close out your "show" with one memorable tag line that spoke to a greater cause – one bigger than you or your ideas?

A passion for a mission is incredibly attractive to an audience. It can also be a total turn-off if handled incorrectly. In the case of Bob Barker, he closed each episode out with that sentiment. However, if during every game, every interaction with his contestants, and every interview he did, he was bringing up the various issues with pet overpopulation, it would cause fatigue and tune-out with even the most loyal of his audience. Instead, Barker did it in a way that resonated with his audience, almost as throwaway as the credits closed. This was not "thrown away" because he did not really care about the issue. He cared very much. He waited until the very end of the program to ensure that was the last thing the audience came away with. It was so important to him that he wanted the audience to remember it and it became engrained in our pop culture long after his time on the game show passed. Today, our society spays and neuters pets almost by default. It is counter to the norm to have pets who are breedable if one is not specifically breeding animals.

Finding a greater cause, mission, purpose, or focus can help grow your reach and your brand. Like-minded loyalists are the building blocks of media relevance. Finding a core audience that speaks to our values and to whom we can speak about those values is what sets many content creators, especially in the social change space of social media, apart from others.

The most important thing about this is that the cause, mission, and purpose of your journey must be authentic to you, important to you, and something in which you truly believe. This should be your underlying passion or the change you want to affect in this world. This should not necessarily be your entire focus, just as I explained with Bob Barker. It does not have to be a specific group, organization, or charity. However, it should be a lens through which you view a topic and a filter through which you analyze content.

The first question to ask yourself is, "why am I doing this?".

If your hope is to become "viral", famous, wealthy, etc., I would suggest you dig a little deeper. While those goals are not altogether corrupt, in absence of a much bigger purpose, they are self-serving and superficial. Having a platform, an audience, influence, and reach is a gift not to be taken lightly. It comes with a great power AND a greater responsibility to leave the space better than before you entered it.

It is true that not everyone in the social media space seems to have this greater responsibility and purpose in mind, and many of the top social media "celebrities" may not seem to have a "mission", per se. Audiences can detect this disingenuous nature of clout chasing for the sake of growing followers, likes, and vanity metrics like someone attempting to notch a high score on an arcade game. Sometimes notching your initials on that top-scorers list after the is a mark of pride. After all, it took a lot of work (and quarters) to achieve that. However, many simply want infamy, the stamp of approval, and bragging rights, just as with social media. I would argue this is not the path to pursue for a content creator seeking longevity and a legacy.

We can do great work with fame and fortune, yes. But we can also affect great change with our properly crafted words and messaging. Fame and fortune are fluid. Change is constant. Progress takes passion and dedication to the mission, whatever that mission is. The desire for fame and fortune are corruptible. This is where you see many content creators "selling out" or "chasing clout". Having that dream of becoming more than you are is not as corrupt. Your motivation and intent behind that dream and the steps you are willing to take to achieve that dream is where it becomes a slippery slope. Having a much bigger, greater-than-you purpose for putting yourself out there can help keep you in check as a creator and as you create content that aligns with your values and mission.

IDENTIFYING YOUR TARGET AUDIENCE

Once you've sharpened your online persona, establishing a character that does not appear as fake or a put-on with your audience, and you have identified your greater mission for your journey, some thought needs to go into your preferred target audience.

We do not always have the luxury of choosing who relates to our personality and content. However, the idea of steering your social media ship through the choppy and crowded waters of the online world of short attention spans and muddled nuance is important. For example, early in my college career, I wanted to be a high school history teacher. For me, I did not want to be surrounded by young children all day and the elementary-and-middle-school curriculum was below my comfort level of how I wanted to spend my days. In other words, I felt like high school students would be more capable of picking up what I was putting down in the way I was comfortable delivering my message. Eventually, I found broadcasting and abandoned not only my teaching dreams, but the idea of selecting my audience completely.

My initial interest was Alternative Rock radio or News/Talk. Those formats are incredibly competitive and not always financially rewarding or stable. During college, mostly due to geography, I found myself in the country radio format. I had little knowledge of country music at first, but I seemed to have a knack for programming to that audience. I found that the audience was loyal and passionate about the music and lifestyle. The only problem was, I did not like the music, and I sure did not like or live the lifestyle. In fact, very little about the audience did I relate to on a personal level. Still, I was able to program radio stations that performed well, and I was able to host shows that performed well, too. In some cases, I played up the fact that I did not live the lifestyle of my audience. Some of that worked, some of it did not. However, the bigger issue overall was that I was not in my comfort zone for most of my broadcasting career. I did not give myself any clearly defined direction early on other than "get a job" and "start my career", so I hopped on the first train out of the station.

I spent the better part of two decades in radio broadcasting, all of that as an on-air personality, most of it programming radio stations, and most of that programming the country format. Had I been afforded the opportunity to hand-pick my target audience, I am certain it would not have been the country music audience. Without sounding critical or judgmental, I simply had little in common with them, and selling authenticity was not always easy. I had to search to find my authentic voice, despite being opposed to much of what defines the rural or country lifestyle. I had to mask my disdain for some elements of that culture, which I am certain did not play well or as genuine. While I came to appreciate the music, I never embraced "country livin'". In the end, when I walked away from my radio career, all those years and all the work I spent building a name for myself in the industry, with an audience, did not translate to my current

40

ambitions. Very little did, in fact. So much so, between being the cultural fish out of water and the years spent in automotive retail before launching my current journey, I did not have a loyal core audience of followers or fans to draw from. I left the radio industry with very little fan capital. Those are the loyal fans who would follow you wherever you go. In terrestrial broadcast radio, some of that lost fan capital is a given, especially pre-internet. However, by the time I retired from radio in 2012, my fan capital was unnurtured and unrefined. I never thought I would leave the radio industry while I was doing radio, and the idea of listeners following me "town to town, up and down the dial" was not even possible early in my radio broadcasting career. When I decided to relaunch my career in the public eye, many of those who listened to me would find that this new, authentic me was not in line with their ideals or values. In other words, if they knew and liked me back then, most of them would not like me for me without being on their favorite radio station. I had to start from scratch with this newly defined authenticity and pursuit of my dreams.

For you, choosing your target audience is something you can do rather easily in the modern world of search engine optimization, algorithms, and hashtags. Clearly defining WHO you are and WHAT you are about will pave the way for a clearer picture of to whom you will be speaking. Look beyond the now into the future. Imagine, down the road, how you might pivot your content and platform, if necessary. If you are building a platform based on a social issue that is of immediate concern, what happens once that issue is resolved or no longer the hot topic? How would you deal with that space being saturated with other creators just as passionate and driven for change?

A narrow or broad approach can matter in the longer term. Just like with my own example, my audience was very narrow for most of my professional life. When I left the radio industry, having no fan capital from which to build a foundation of support for my new endeavors or my newly defined message and mission, pivoting became difficult because I was not going to another radio station or format but transitioning into another space altogether – one where I would be highly critical of some of the traits and qualities with which my former audience might have identified.

Narrow now but broader beyond is my philosophy. When it comes to social change, my focus might be on a few specific social issues or major greater talking points, but much broader is the message of ethics, to which most people can relate. I might be talking about women's rights, LGBTQIA+ rights, or the rights of people of color in America, but ultimately, big picture, I am talking about the ethics of opinion.

Taking my couponing content creator example from earlier, if the narrow now is coupon clippers and bargain hunters, then the broader beyond might be budget efficiency, saving for a rainy day, economic realities, etc. Then, if the day comes when couponing and searching for discounts is no longer trendy, pivoting to another focus within that space becomes much easier. You have identified not only your narrow-now audience as those who use coupons and discount codes, but also your broader-beyond audience, which might be meal planning, recycling/reusing, sustainability, self-sufficiency, etc.

A clearly defined purpose in your intent to be a content creator or social media influencer is as important as the clearly defined purpose of your message and your platform. This is an important journey for you as well as your audience. You might have several or many passion points you want to "be about". In all that, find the connection, and focus on that. You read about pivoting's pitfalls, and it applies to this as well. Standing up for one thing, then moving on to another cause might leave your audience feeling as if you have "moved on" from what was so important to you before, and even make them wonder if your concern or dedication for that was authentic or performative. However, if you Big Picture your cause, mission, or purpose early in your process, pivoting is easier. Just as with my own example! Ethics and moral dilemmas – forming opinions from the highest ground of reason possible – are at the heart of most everything I discuss. Shifting gears from one issue to another is not as jarring for me or my audience, as that is a broader cause that touches almost every issue I discuss.

DUNNING-KRUGER VERSUS THE AUTHORITY OF EXPERTISE

Charles Darwin was quoted as saying, "Ignorance more frequently begets confidence than does knowledge". In other content and context, I have spoken about the term Academic Confidence. This is where if a student feels confident about the work they are doing, they are more likely to improve and grow than if they feel like they are struggling or failing. In school settings, this idea encourages educators to reconsider grading methodologies, not to pass students who have not mastered a subject, but to build a system that encourages the process of learning and expressing mastery rather than a simple "Pass/Fail and move on to the next topic" paradigm. Students who may struggle then have little incentive to keep trying and will continue to struggle with everything that builds off that topic they did not pass. However, with an understanding of Academic Confidence, students are encouraged more for their efforts and trying, thus they will work harder to obtain mastery of that topic. If you miss 100% of the shots you try, eventually, even trying becomes tedious and future shots are missed more out of frustration than failure. Keeping with the basketball analogies, lower that 10-foot basket to 8 feet and work on the mechanics of shooting, then gradually raise the goal as the student improves, until their goal is at that regulation 10-foot height, and they can compete more equitably.

44

The benefit of this approach to teaching and learning is that the student will have more confidence in what they are doing. The downside, in the basketball example, is when that student feels TOO confident and coddled on that lower, 8-foot goal and stops trying to raise the standard. They have lowered the goal permanently – thus, lowering the standard of excellence in themselves and eventually, their expectations of excellence from others. Just like misery, mediocrity loves company, too.

Excellence is making a higher percentage of basketball shots on the professional-standard of 10-feet. While they may look good draining baskets in their driveway, once they are out among the real experts of the game, their lower standards, settling for that 8-foot goal, will be exposed. In the athletic space, one does not practice free throws for a day and accepts that whatever their completion percentage after that is, is forever. However, in academic settings, this is too often the case. A student has an assignment and scores a 78/100. Scoring higher is possible if they can practice more. However, academically, for so long, the rush was to accept that initial grade and move on to the next topic. That student could have been sent back to the free throw line, told specifically what caused the 22-points to be deducted, and have them try again. The next draft of that assignment might result in an 86/100. This is not giving the student the answers to the test. This is teaching the student how to master and show mastery of subjects. Now, imagine how much more information a student might absorb retrying that assignment to achieve a higher score than if they just accept the 78 and move on to the next topic.

In the social media space, there are many self-professed experts ready to share their seemingly vast knowledge about any number of topics. With this comes the Latin phrase, "caveat emptor", or buyer beware. Anyone can say anything today with few in the audience ready to dig deep and validate the claims of expertise. Some of this is deliberate deception. However, mental health is to blame for at least a portion of this phenomenon.

With casual conversations, if we feel left out or in over our heads, there may be a temptation to speak up, express yourself. Everyone has an opinion, and the social media space has become the place where everyone can exercise their voice. Whether just trying to keep up with the discussion or blatantly misrepresenting one's competence or authority, the result does not change much. It can cause dissatisfaction in the audience and embarrassment or worse for the content creator.

Psychologists David Dunning and Justin Kruger researched the phenomenon that was named after them: The Dunning-Kruger Effect. There is a much deeper psychological definition, but summed up, this is where someone believes themselves to be an expert on a topic when they are not. The individual may lack the self-awareness to admit to even themselves that their knowledge, understanding, or competence in a topic only goes so far, so they attempt to fake it until they make it.

Often, the individual lacks the cognitive self-awareness to understand their own limitations. We see this in livestreams where guests are brought up randomly, regardless of the topic being discussed with no talk or consideration of what makes them qualified to speak on that topic. However, in professional media, this would never happen. The professional producers of the professional show go to great lengths to ensure the person being paneled or platformed on their program has the gravitas, credentials, and experience to speak on the subject. When the host moves on to a different subject, they move on to a new guest who specializes in the new subject. They rarely keep the previous guest on to comment on something out of their arena.

I ask the question quite often, "why should I listen to you?". This can sound offensive to some who believe their opinion is valid regardless of whether they have done any work in forming that opinion or not. In fact, should we not all ask this of anyone we allow to voice an opinion in our spaces? The wonderful thing about social media is anyone can have a platform. That is also the downside of social media. There are no warnings, disclaimers, disclosures or accountability.

One might ask, "well, then why should anyone listen to you, Josh?". Maybe they shouldn't. Maybe they are more learned and experienced than I and I should be learning from them! I acknowledge that my education and experience, while vast, is humble. I attended state university, nothing Ivy League. My high school grade point average was 2.86. That is not to say I did not learn a lot or that I was a bad student. I attended a school that cared as much about me as I did the school. However, my life has been spent learning new things, studying various subjects. But no one knows how little I know more than I.

The Dunning-Kruger Effect, in a manner of thinking, is lacking the internal firewall of protection that tells you, "Ok, this is as much as you can say on this topic". It is the ego's doubling-and-tripling down on our authority on whatever given subject. One does not even have to believe that they are "better than", "smarter than", or even "equal to" actual experts. The Dunning-Kruger Effect is quite simply the individual's over-inflation of their abilities and knowledge without recognition or acknowledgement of their own limitations in that area.

Dunning and Kruger's findings were published in 1999. It appeared to suggest a cyclical effect I spoke about with Academic Confidence and the basketball free throws. Confidence without competence hinders the individual's ability to recognize how much work they have to do to be as knowledgeable as they think they are. That confidence breeds arrogance and entitlement that halts growth and learning.

Nearly two decades later, additional research into The Dunning-Kruger Effect would reveal some alarming details about topics not included in the initial study: Areas of business, healthcare and medicine, and politics. According to Brittanica, this study, focused on those in the United States, showed that those who know little, express a lot, especially the more biased or loyal that person is to one partisan political ideology.

We saw this showcased on display for the world to see during the COVID-19 pandemic of 2020, when it seemed like everyone was a virologist and vaccine expert. The social media space was littered with those expressing opinions on complex matters of science by those with limited knowledge, experience, or expertise. We also have seen this with political issues, social issues, and various topics in the "culture wars". Those who have little understanding, perspective, or knowledge on a topic being the loudest voices. The Dunning-Kruger Effect.

Examine your own expertise – the areas in which you can speak from authority without the risk of being called out as a fraud. Respect and understand the limitations of your own knowledge. Work hard to fill those gaps or to network and find your verified expert guests to speak on those subjects. Remember, you do not have to be an expert or authority in topics with which you are not comfortable. However, it is important to avoid stepping up to the camera or microphone to express an idea that you have not thoroughly researched.

Research, in social media, is misused like the word debate. There are very few true debates on social media. There are discussions and debacles, but few true academic debates, by the rules of debate. Just as with the Inigo Montoya Effect of the word "debate", people will use the term "research" as a substitute for typing a question into a search engine.

"You keep using that word. I do not think it means what you think it means".

THE UGLY TRUTHS

The fact is that most people do not earn a significant living, or income, through social media. Most social media content creators do this out of a hobby, a passion, or the sacrifice of now in hopes of an eventual payoff once they 'blow up'. The ugly truth is you probably will never 'blow up'. Most creators who "go viral" barely pop. If they do, so many are here today, gone tomorrow. In sales we called that going from Hero to Zero. As the defined sales period ended to start anew each month, the sales staff would set a goal to achieve and if they exceeded that at the end of the month, there was little time for celebration. The next day started a whole new month where they were at zero.

Social media can seem like that. It becomes discouraging and emotionally disincentivizing. One often might feel the mental or physical effects of trying to remain relevant in such a toxic and unhealthy environment. The struggles one encounters in the journey of social media content creation are innumerable and subject to the individual, niche, and specific platform on which they are sharing content.

This is not an easy journey. Nor is this a journey I recommend for most. In acting and entertainment, I get rejected multiple times a day, countless times a year. The reality of my career is that I do not make most of the shots I attempt. Most entertainers don't. We audition against dozens, if not hundreds, of other performers on each project. Sometimes those roles are filled before we even try for it. In other cases, we do not look the part, the person they have already cast is much taller or shorter and the on-screen dynamic would not play as well on camera, they have cast the children before the adults and are trying to match looks, or any number of reasons that do not always have to do with the actor, their talent, or what they could bring to the project. There are so many factors out of our control as performers that it simply does not make sense to allow silent rejection to dictate your path. Silent rejection is where you do not get the opportunity, but you get no constructive criticism as to why you were not selected. You just know you did not get picked, and that can hurt. In fact, there are any number of reasons possible, but in absence of those facts, anxiety steps in to fill those gaps. That self-doubt will hinder your success, growth, and confidence. Prepare to lose more than you win, and you should be fine.

In the end, just as with sales, it is just a numbers game. Throw spaghetti to the wall and see what sticks. There are so many clichés that apply here, so I will spare you. The important thing is to have a clearly defined idea of who you are, what you are about, to whom you want to communicate that, and a realistic expectation of rejection. Post, post, post! Do not concern yourself with negativity unless that negativity stems from a legitimate mistake you have made. Then, simply do your best to make amends, learn from it, and keep posting.

Do not take it personally. Just hold your head up and try, try again.

Mental health is another factor altogether and we cannot discuss the ugly truths of social media influence without acknowledging the drastic toll the vitriol, hate, trolling, and attacks can take on your spirit. Earlier I used the term emotionally disincentivizing, which is the most accurate way I have heard this journey described. The time you spend on that video you are sure will make a difference, the effort you put in to edit it just right, the scrutiny you show analyzing the background music or effects, and then it barely moves the needle. For most content creators, even if it is not about the vanity metrics of engagement, we still want our ideas to be heard. What can be worse is when your detractors target your content or your account, reporting you for violations you did not commit, attempting to "take you down". For the troll, this is a trophy. For the person who has nothing, something is everything. What can be even worse than troll takedowns are feelings like the platform itself has targeted you and your content, hindering your growth deliberately.

In my personal experience, my life has been threatened repeatedly by white nazionalists and violent Confederate insurrectionists hell bent on ushering in an agenda of fascism in America. I have had them attempt to organize plots to murder me, attack me, or invade my home. These terrorist organizations like the III%ers, The Proud Boys, Moms 4 Liberty, Patriot Front, and more – and actual, literal Nazis, have taken to the dark web with plots, threats, and doxing my personal information and that of my family. This, all because I stand against white supremacy and bigotry. I have spent thousands of dollars on security for my home and property and that of those close to me, body armor to protect me on the protest lines, and even methods of self-defense. My neighborhood was vandalized, with terrorists spray-painting political propaganda and slurs on the road in front of my home. All of this is because I stepped up on the soapbox and took the spotlight of the public eye to speak very important truths on social media. It is true that none of that should have happened, but you need to understand the risks associated with choosing to be in the public eye. Even if your content is not as socially, culturally, or politically polarizing as my own, understand that very sick and twisted, mentally ill people exist in the world and those people pose a very real risk to you as a content creator.

All that notwithstanding, even the threats, pressures, and stresses that come with trying to exist in this world off social media, then to trying to make a difference on social media among the static and the clutter, can be overwhelming and mentally or emotionally exhausting. I encourage therapy and a dedication to mental health, planning downtime and breaks, recording more content than you post daily, so that when you do take a break, you have a cache of content from which to pull, post, and keep your algorithm from growing stagnant. Remember, you do not have to interact or engage to post. You can always catch up. It is also ok to take a breather from everything else on social media EXCEPT your content. This is your platform; you make the rules. Most of them anyway.

Look out for your own well-being. Do not get pulled into the middle school cafeteria drama of social media. Rise above the toxicity and stay true to your message, mission, and yourself.

YOU _ARE_ A MEDIA PERSONALITY

Keep your ego in check. Do not let a little success go to your head. However, it is important that you take a hard look at yourself and acknowledge what you want. You must be humble, realistic, but honest with yourself. The odds are that you won't "get noticed" and "make it big". That's just math. However, if the journey and goal is important enough to you that you are willing to not make money or achieve life-changing fame, then you are in this for the right reasons.

There is a level of selling-out, or compromising, one must confront when taking steps in each career. Those are the boundaries of your own design based on your ethics, morals, and values. As an independent voice actor and performer for film, commercials, and television, there are some things I simply will not put my brand on. Alcohol, tobacco, firearms are some easy industries as examples. Politics, religion, and exploitation of others. Maybe yours are different and you might want to put some thought into what your "price" is for bending your boundaries.

For me, I do not consume alcohol and tobacco for various reasons, so I cannot rationalize profiting from encouraging others to do so. I do political content, but I do not do political advertising. I might do an issues-based political ad, under certain circumstances, but a campaign ad for a political figure is something I often do not feel comfortable with.

These thoughts are part of defining yourself as a media personality, on any level.

The most important thing is to understand and acknowledge that you ARE a media personality. Own that. Denial will make it easier to compromise your values, ethics, and boundaries because it will be easier to sell yourself short, dismissing yourself as not important. If you have an audience, you have importance. We hold the power of influence in our hands with social media. That is not to over-inflate our self-importance, but to acknowledge that it is real so we can better understand our responsibilities and roles in this greater media landscape.

Most platforms today provide the opportunity to "go live" or livestream your content real-time. This alone takes social media and makes it the equivalent of a broadcast network, with you having your own channel on that network. You can schedule your livestreams or fly by the seat of your pants. You can dictate a level of professionalism and ethical guidelines, or you can simply go with the flow. However, looking at a given platform as some twisted hybrid of a college radio station and public access TV, but with the potential global reach of a legitimate broadcast network can be eye opening!

In this regard, your "show" has no censors, standards and practices, or management breathing down your throat barking about ratings and advertisers. You might have taken a deep sigh of relief and thought, "thank goodness for that". Having worked in the industry, I would echo that sentiment. However, my experience also tells me that there is no support system there either, ensuring that the proper steps are taken to be responsible with the platform, or that the best strategies for growth are implemented.

You have your own channel, your own show, and a network who allows you to go Lights, Camera, Action whenever you feel like it. If you do not see the gravity of responsibility in that, I might argue that you should take a step back, very seriously consider it, and reevaluate the first part of this book in relation to where you belong in this space. The gatekeepers may not be there any longer standing in the way of you walking into a television or radio station and saying whatever you want, but we are today's gatekeepers with the onus of all the responsibility they used to shoulder on us. The internet is forever and there is no seven-second delay safety net beneath us. It is just the content creator flying high on the social media trapeze for all to see. If your trick does not land, you could be left plummeting toward the dust like a wily coyote.

POOF!

Meep, Meep, my friends. Meep, Meep.

And, in that fall, there may be no getting back up. Do not risk your platform, your relevance, your audience, or your opportunity. Take the opportunity seriously. Take yourself seriously. Take the responsibility seriously. There is a tremendous upside to knowing you "made it" the right way.

Section 2:

RESPONSIBILITY, DUTIES, AND OBLIGATIONS

So, you are a social media personality! That means you have the potential to reach hundreds, thousands, or even millions of followers! Results may vary. As a former television and radio personality with a bachelor's degree in communication and a master's in teaching, I can tell you there is a significant amount of academic coursework that goes into teaching young, aspiring media talent about things like legality, ethics, responsibility, and the importance of holding to some standards.

Today, anyone with a device and Wi-Fi can be a social media personality. It's never been easier to BE heard. This section will help you understand the importance and obligations that come with wielding that kind of power of influence.

BROADCASTING VERSUS SOCIAL MEDIA

When one speaks of broadcasting, we often think about radio frequencies and television waves. AM, FM, UHF, and VHF. To the Federal Communications Commission, this is accurate. However, while the legislation and regulations for we, the creator, can be a little muddy at times, harkening back to the age-old philosophies that kept those entities on the air for over a century might be a good place from which to build a foundation.

The definition of broadcasting is more aligned with the dissemination of information for the masses, the general public, at-large. Narrowcasting is the opposite. It is the delivery of information, but to a smaller, more niche audience. That certainly sounds more like social media, doesn't it?

The biggest difference, in legislation and regulation, comes from the fact that radio and television, due to broadcast technology, are intrusive media. Meaning they are put out there for everyone and all one needs is a receiving device. There is no firewall otherwise to prevent those messages from being delivered to the public. Anyone with a radio or TV, with the technology to receive broadcast signals, and within the range of the signal, can consume broadcast radio and television.

For most of the last century, the FCC has regulated only broadcast radio and broadcast television, local and network in the ways we think of the FCC standing guard over things like obscenity, standards and practices, etc. However, those subscription services, like cable television, which rose to popularity in the 1980's, satellite radio, which became relevant in the 90's, and the internet, which became the new frontier of media in the years prior to the turn of the century, have always been exempt from much of that regulation. The reason being, "caveat emptor". Buyer beware!

The consumer subscribes to these services. Therefore, there is the dreaded Terms of Service, which basically lays the responsibility for whatever is on those services more on the consumers plate than in front of the service, or up the line of content creation. While there are some rules and regulations, the ones that SHOULD affect us, simply don't apply to non-intrusive media, like subscription-based services.

This is why cable programming can go farther in what they show, say, and do than network programming.

In many regards, social media is more narrowcasting than broadcasting, since it is designed for a more niche, and selective audience. However, social media IS broadcasting, as it is easily accessible to most consumers. You have the signal (Wi-Fi), and the receiver (phones). No more does the creator need a studio with expensive cameras, lights, and a satellite in the air with their logo on it to broadcast. They only need a phone and a few bars.

The argument might be that, just as with cable and satellite radio, one needs a subscription of some sort to access the internet. If not the internet, then at the very least the apps one uses to access the internet. For that slippery slope, I would suggest not leaning toward the side of justification rationale, rather than to stand on the side of safety – for you and for others.

The reality is that technically speaking or practically speaking, social media apps have shifted the societal and social landscape in ways sociologists will be analyzing for centuries to come. For better or worse, social media has changed us and I believe a great deal of the 'worse' part of that is the floodgates of accessibility were opened with most not understanding the power and responsibility that comes with that access.

The idea to always keep in mind is that social media has the potential to reach anyone who stumbles across your content. If it is on the internet, available for the public, then we simply must consider the uncomfortable truth of who might be able to consume it. Once upon a time, broadcasters recognized that and held to standards that prevented the spread of propaganda, misinformation, and hate speech.

Today, the public no longer has that protection – at the cost of a warped misinterpretation of our country's First Amendment – which has absolutely nothing to do with social media whatsoever.

ADVERTISING AND AUTHENTICITY

When one reaches a certain level of relevance or popularity on social media, there may be options to capitalize on that. "Cash-in" as some might say. "Sell-out" as others might warn. There is no right answer that fits all here. This is a standard you set for yourself. There are content creators who seek the platform because of the perks that might come with it. For those, it is not necessarily disingenuous. The idea is that they can just be themselves in a space and build a following and supplement the time and effort it takes to do that with product endorsements, testimonials, or what is called UGC (User-Generated Content), or ads that are designed to trick the audience into thinking it is actual social media content.

There are so many opportunities today to find some tangible benefits of being on social media. Many platforms have programs designed for their content creators. There are talent agencies that specialize in social media content creators and influencers, who connect the advertiser to the creator. Seeking to take advantage of this requires some searching and due diligence to ensure you are not being scammed or taken advantage of.

My first piece of advice on this subject is, when you hit a certain audience threshold, and that is different for each platform, then start looking for social media agencies and inquire within. There is no easy way to do it. Some agencies may not take new clients if they have enough of "you" on their roster. That is not a bad thing, except if you are the one left out. That means that the agency respects their roster enough to recognize bringing more people in will mean fewer opportunities for their established clients. That is the representation game. You might find representation right away. Ask for social media and camera opportunities, as well. You might find a proactive agent who sees something more than just social media in your future. You might get to audition for television commercials or more! Always think big-picture and long-game.

Now, the medicine to go down with all that sugar.

There is a responsibility that goes with advertising, endorsing, testifying, or influencing others. If you have charisma, confidence, and communication skills, you can be in sales. Cars, homes, merchandise, insurance, it does not matter. For the person who has the "It Factor", they just must want it and want to learn how to use "it".

The standards and ethics you choose to use on social media are completely up to the individual. Your audience will experience fatigue if you use your platform to sell to them too much. Your audience will grow bored and maybe annoyed if it seems you are using your platform to sell just anything. The audience demands authenticity, on some level. If everything you show them and share with them bears similar importance, excitement, and verbiage, then is any of it that good? Or are you just a slick salesperson trying to cash out while the cashin's good?

Your audience will know. Do not underestimate them.

Do not ever lie, misrepresent, or manipulate to sell a product or brand on your platform. The few hundred dollars you might make now is not worth it in the long run. A careless, short-sighted approach to your online brand's career can be costly down the road. Beyond the legal implications of it, there are the ethical and practical disadvantages that could cost you your platform and/or future opportunities.

It might be wise to define a set of standards for yourself and your platform. What you do not want is for you, your platform, or your brand is to "take off" and then you have products, brands, or ideas that you have promoted which do not necessarily match your values or image. Be very scrutinous of the horse you hitch your wagon to. It can be hard to get off that ride once you are on it.

THE RESPONSIBILITY OF MASS COMMUNICATION

Responsibility is the wet blanket of social media content creation. Who wants to consider right and wrong, duty and obligation, responsibility and recklessness when making videos? Still, this is a very important idea to discuss. My understanding of this responsibility is likely different than yours. Mine is filtered through academic education and years of experience in the communication industries. I see things through many perspectives when it comes to social media content creation and social influence.

The most important thing to remember is whatever it is you want to say, think of the worst-case scenario of someone hearing that and then back down your reasoning from there. Assuming the worst can keep you from making a grievous error out of emotion or ignorance. Forming opinions before you have all the information, or enough information to be sure that opinion is one strong enough to defend, can cause problems in many social media spaces.

While most platforms allow you to hold content you have created for posting later, many creators simply get the idea, turn on the camera, start talking, and out into the ether it goes! How much consideration do you put into your ideas, as far as how others might receive it in ways you did not intend? That simply is not a filter most amateur content creators apply in their process. Still, with our language so fluid right now, as we phase out more and more toxic, abusive, and hurtful language, imagine saying something in the moment that, TO YOU, does not sound offensive, but to another group with whom you have little exposure, it is racially or otherwise hurtful? Your intent was not to use that word or phrase to hurt anyone. Yet now you have other creators making videos based off yours calling you out. That is a mess you do not want to clean up.

Acknowledging the importance of responsibility of communicating to the masses will help you create better, more reliable content that hits the mark more often. Your passion, personality, and purpose will not matter the moment you cross a line of acceptable social boundaries, and those are ever-changing.

Beyond just that example, there are the responsibilities that come with endorsing products, individuals, or ideas that can influence and affect others. Putting at least some thought into how you want to conduct yourself and which processes and standards through which you choose to create content will set you apart from the individual who flies by the seat of their pants. While that may come off as initially appealing and authentic, that appeal of authenticity is a powder keg by a campfire. The untrained individual, with no understanding or acknowledgement of the responsibility of mass communication, runs the risk of igniting that, resulting in blowing up everything they've worked for.

Another responsibility to acknowledge is not only your own mental health as the content creator or influencer, but the mental health of your audience. As I have discussed with Dunning-Kruger, authority, and expertise, there are many in your audience who may have personality disorders, or other mental health issues that can put you at risk. While extreme examples are rare, there are risks with putting yourself out there for public consumption. Some of those I covered from my own personal experience.

Parasocial relationships are something to be aware of in the social media space. When I was on television, early on, it was on a micro-scale. More local cable access than network news, I still felt the pressure of parasocial relationships. I did not know what it was, but it made me uncomfortable, nonetheless. Today, I know that parasocial relationships are those relationships people feel they have with an individual whom they do not know personally. This is a negative side-effect of the kind of authenticity and relatability one needs to build a loyal following.

While I experienced this much more during my radio career, the experiences as a small, rural news anchor at 19 years old traumatized me. I would go out with my friends, shopping, or to dine out, and people would come up to me and strike up conversations. While that in and of itself can be a harmless intrusion on privacy or personal boundaries, I have always tried to accommodate in the best and most polite ways I can in the given scenario. Many do not see the intrusion, only their opportunity to meet someone they have seen on television or listened to on the radio.

For some in your audience, you will come into their lives, casually, in their social media space, and communicate with them. They might relate to you so much they feel closer to you, even if you are unaware of their existence. Local media has been built on parasocial relationships. Your local news anchors, radio personalities, and other public figures rely on a safe level of that to garner the support they need to be successful. If you feel like you know the news anchors, you are more likely to tune in and watch. If the morning radio hosts are "your friends", then you feel like you are letting them down by not listening. Some of this is manipulation. Some of this is strategic. I was personally never comfortable with fake relationships, so when someone approached me carrying on like they knew me when I just met them, it sent up a red flag. Not all who struggle with these boundaries are dangerous, but stepping into the social media space, into the public eye, where you are communicating a broad message to the masses, do not be surprised when some of them feel a closer relationship to you than you have. This is not something to mock or manipulate, either. Often there may be psychological issues, mental health diagnoses, or other factors that we are not aware of. Respecting healthy boundaries for ourselves while being compassionate to others is the best strategy for safety. However, do not ignore warning signs or red flags.

Don't be seduced by the vanity metrics of likes and follows. Stay true to yourself but be responsible and mindful of everyone's safety in the social media space. Be especially mindful of your own safety.

ETHICS AND INTEGRITY IN SOCIAL MEDIA

Social media, as we have learned, does not receive the same level of scrutiny as broadcast radio and television. Nor do the standards and practices apply. Things like ethics and integrity were once the standard, especially for journalism, news, and information media. The ads might have skirted the lines of misrepresentation, and when they did, and got caught, they were forced to use disclaimers. Social media has no such disclaimers except for the unspoken overall disclaimer that social media itself is a vast wasteland where anything is possible – good and bad.

Journalistic integrity is an idea that has lasted longer than broadcast news was a technology. There has been a longstanding code of ethics to which professional journalists have adhered for many years. During much of the 20th century, these practices were what kept the delivery of news information and editorialized opinion commentary separated in the consumer's mind. Today, that separation has eroded as much as the code of ethics.

In the Middle Ages, the three estates recognized were, respectively, the royals or nobles, the church, and the people. In more modern times, the press has often been referred to as "The 4th Estate", separate from those other entities, acting independently for the people. For this reason, the press has been considered one of the most important cornerstones of American democracy, because it has always been held to a higher standard of being factual, objective, and independent of the government. In fact, the First Amendment of the Constitution recognizes the Freedom of the Press, as defined, as the guarantee the government will not impede the press and their informing of the people – that the government will not pursue the press out of retribution for what the press reports.

Social media is in no way The 4th Estate. The standards, ethics, integrity, and protections are not there. However, to the consumer, the social media landscape gets awash in this grey area due the fact that so many amateur content creators have become a source for news, information, commentary, and perspective – Moreso than even their local broadcast or print journalism sources.

The difference between these two sources for information is the code of ethics used to discover, investigate, and report that information. While many different countries and cultures vary on the specific code of ethics they use for reporting news and information, in the United States, a code of ethics has been recognized for well over a century and still today by organizations such as The Society of Professional Journalists and The Ethical Journalism Network, whose respective codes bear similarities.

I suggest content creators embrace a hybrid of these codes for their own philosophy on ethics and integrity. Some of my suggestions are based, in part, on some of the well-respected and established codes of ethics in journalism because, as content creators, we either value truth or we do not. We either act in ethical ways or we are unethical. There is no middle ground, I'm afraid. So, let's consider some philosophies that might help you on social media.

Seek Truth and Report It

Whatever niche you choose for your platform, if it is information-based or centered around current events, journalists have traditionally lived by a primary rule. If there is a story, find it. Find out the truth. Report that truth to whomever will listen.

The ethical concerns come from the methods one uses to find the story, determine what is truth and what is conjecture, and then the way they report or deliver that information. Just as with evidence in a criminal case, there are ways one can corrupt a crime scene, compromising the evidence's reliability. Our constitutional rights do not always apply on social media, but we can work to hold ourselves to some standards of ethics, even if no one else is forcing us.

Truth in reporting, honesty in communicating, and transparency in gathering of that information is the highest standard. If it does not pass the "is it true" test, do we need to be saying it?

How do you ensure you are reporting, delivering, or creating content that is truthful and accurate information? It is as easy as 1, 2, 3!

With whatever information you receive, your obligation is due diligence to ensure it is accurate <u>before</u> you share it. You do this by seeking out three indisputable, independent, unbiased sources of that same information. In today's corporatized and homogenized world of infotainment, that might seem like an insurmountable task, but it is one we still must endure.

Sometimes, your initial source is a viable first confirmable source. Then, you need only to seek that information elsewhere to validate its accuracy, or at very least that reputable sources have also vetted the information. Even if, and maybe especially if, your first source of information is a major news network or reputable brand, your duty is to still seek triple confirmation of that information's accuracy. There are no shortcuts where ethics are concerned. A simple internet search can provide additional information. Beware of opinion blogs, clearly biased reporting, and do some homework on which media outlets and organizations are owned by which parent companies and how those companies lean, politically. If the information you want to create content on is impacted by bias, improper reporting, or missing or misleading information, that can impact your accurate reporting of the information, thus impacting your reputation as a content creator.

Do No Harm

In journalism, this principle is, at least in part, about protecting sources, while considering the public safety and social temperature. In social media, those things are important considerations. With regard to protecting sources, maybe a better way to translate this to the social space would be not fabricating details to help solidify one's point – creating an anonymous source to justify one's position.

Moreover, the idea here is that with everything you do, do so with as pure intent as possible. Even if your intent is to do an epic takedown video for someone who has crossed a line, is your intent to cause that person harm or to report on an injustice with hopes someone takes notice? The former can be litigiously dangerous and might result in the creator being held legally liable for that harm caused. The latter is more altruistic, less affected by personal bias, and less corrupted by personal agendas.

Acting Independently with Objectivity

When creating content, especially if it is news or information based and you want to uphold a sense of ethical integrity, avoid bias, prejudice, and opinion. These may influence the kind of content you create, the lean of your messaging, and the unique personality you bring to the information, but they should never corrupt the process of scrutinizing the information. Omission of important information or inclusion of false-or-misinformation to suit an agenda is unethical by journalism standards and should be something even an amateur or, especially, aspiring professional in the social media space avoids as well.

With whatever you do, say, and create, do so independently, with authenticity and objectivity. Apply a pragmatic filter to your content and the truth will shine. There is a lot of room for perspective in that truth in how you frame it, but the truth itself should be untouched, available for your audience in a clear and understandable way. Starting from a place independent of bias and prejudice, valuing facts over feelings with an altruistic intent will ensure you are creating content from the highest ethical ground possible. Your audience will recognize and respect that.

Accuracy and Accountability

The principles covered so far all speak to ensuring accuracy in reporting. While many content creators may not look at themselves or what they do as "news", the delivery of information, objective and independent of bias, is theoretically news. It can be received as news by the consumer. Perhaps some might think because their content is more commentary and opinion-driven that accuracy matters less than if they were behind a news desk on network prime time. Regardless of your platform or specific content, sharing information with your audience requires a level of accuracy the audience demands.

Next, is accountability, which is something we do not see as much of in the social media space. Accountability is not apologizing when one makes an error. Accountability is ensuring every step is taken to ensure those errors do not occur before they occur. Then, when an error happens, as is often unavoidable, the creator comes from a more earnest place of making that right with their audience. Accountability is a foundation of ethical integrity. If one holds themselves accountable, then others do not have to work so hard to hold that person accountable.

Mindfulness, Truthfulness, and Maintaining Trust

There is a principle that speaks to causing no harm. Other similar ideas in other journalism circles focus on a sense of humanity and compassion. When creating content, specifically news-and-information based, one should be mindful that all steps are taken to ensure accuracy, reliability, and a reputation for upholding the principles of ethical delivery of information.

In interviews, panel discussions, or what some might refer to as an "online debate", we see ethics and integrity tossed out the window. The host or creator may allow someone of opposite opinion or ideology on their panel or content in the spirit of healthy discourse. In the socio-political social media space, we see a lot of this. Often, the experiment devolves into shouting, elevated tempers, and an audience either tuning out of the drama, or worse, tuning in for the drama. The message is lost either way and any hope of influencing others or affecting change flies out the window with ethics and integrity.

Being mindful of your audience, one might consider that the audience who comes for the information, not necessarily for the fight, might feel negatively affected by the guest's ideas and their ability to voice those ideas so freely, which may be hurtful, hateful, bullying, and misinformation. As a host or content creator the onus is on you to maintain a healthy and productive space for your audience, above all else – even entertainment value. The perceived entertainment value of an online debate/argument is like the suggestion that a huge crowd gathering to watch a fight in a parking lot is more valuable than the crowd watching two friends reunited hugging. The latter may not be as large, exciting, or engaging, but they are there for the right reasons. The fight crowd often does not consider the collateral damage of the incident, just that they enjoy the spectacle. Don't fall into the trap of allowing your platform to become a circus sideshow unless you want to be known as a carnival barker.

Lastly, holding to a standard of truthfulness is vital. Violating the trust of your audience is difficult to overcome. Being known for not being truthful will affect your overall goals of growth. It is important to maintain the trust of your audience, and the audience to which you hope to appeal. You do this through maintaining truth as the highest priority and mindfulness in representing that truth to others.

Consideration of the Greater Good

In everything we do, we, as content creators, should consider the greater good. This poses difficulties because "the greater good" is objective and often comes down to moral dilemmas. There are many examples one could examine. In most cases, there are pros and cons for creating questionable content. Ultimately, it is up to you, the content creator, to decide if it fits your brand and endgame.

An easy example of a nuclear attack might be hyperbolic, but as unlikely as it might be, we can start at unrealistic and then apply that all the way down to the mundane. If you had it on good authority that something was going to happen, but you knew it would wreak chaos for the public, is it your place to assume that responsibility? Well, my argument would be if you do not feel it is your responsibility, leave it for someone else. I know that can seem counterproductive to delivering truthful information, but being first with information is not always best. It has the potential to be a breaking story, but if the content creator breaking that story is not disciplined and trained, at least informed on ethical standards and best practices for maintaining accuracy and integrity, then that story risks breaking the creator, too.

T.H.I.N.K. Test

If you have children, you might have seen a sign at their school that says something like "Before you speak, T.H.I.N.K.". This is something taught to young children early to remember to be mindful of the power of their words and actions. Before you speak, is what you are about to say True, Helpful, Inspiring, Necessary, or Kind?

Reiterating how important fact-based information is, especially in the opinion commentary minefield of social media, T.H.I.N.K. is a valuable acronym to remember that will help you build a strong following. Speaking something as true when one knows it is not or even might not be is irresponsible and, to an audience, unforgivable. I would have to ask why would you want an audience that forgives misleading with misinformation, manipulation, abusive behavior, or lying?

Back to the idea of Do No Harm, remembering that our goal is to leave a positive impact on the world around us, we should lead with intent to be helpful. Sometimes being helpful is not placating the audience or sugar-coating the information. However, the intent in the creator's mind should be mostly altruistic – to be helpful.

People can go anywhere for snark, sarcasm, and social media smackdowns. Is the information you want to deliver necessary? To whom is it important and why? Find a way to make that information or content inspiring. Maybe that is not always possible, but if you use this guideline as a filter through which you view all content, it will help your overall goals.

Kindness might seem to be the most difficult task of all, especially in certain social media spaces. Still, while specific content might be sharp, pointed, or critical, thinking under the umbrella of kindness in creating will make you a stronger content creator and someone with whom a larger audience can and will want to relate.

A HIGHER STANDARD

Observance and implementation of these principles and a respect for ethics and integrity in reporting, or delivering information, will usher in a new, higher standard for you as a content creator, and can impact the social media space on a larger scale as more and more content creators embrace these ideals.

This book, and the information and tools around it, is not intended to be the blueprint for social media success. These are simply suggestions on how you can be a stronger creator with a higher sense of responsibility for what you create and the messages you convey.

As I have mentioned, the social media space, for independent, amateur creators at least, is not one that adheres to a set of ethics, integrity, or standards. It can be a Wild West High Noon shootout of insults, misinformation, and attacks. All the easier it is to fall into the trap so many in that space fall prey to – impulsive and emotional responses.

We cannot control everyone else – or anyone else for that matter. However, as individuals, if we craft our own understanding of boundaries and best practices, and maintain our respect for those new, higher standards, those ideas will catch on, like any other trend, and possibly ethics can "go viral".

Section 3:

CREATING COMPELLING CONTENT

Being a content creator or social media influencer, as you have learned, comes with a great deal of responsibility. This is why finding out who you are and what you are about early on will help you as you create content to ensure you are creating the best and most compelling content possible, from a place of high standards and ethical integrity. Now, let's discuss the actual creation of your content and some things you can do, as a content creator, to make that content stand out. Again, there is very little one can do about the specific algorithms of a given platform, but creating compelling content consistently ensures that in the event you catch that viral wave, you will be ready to not only capitalize on that but ride that wave for much longer.

BRAINSTORMING

The first ideas are rarely the best ideas. In fact, they can be, but that takes training your thought process, almost like muscle memory. After a while, you can begin bypassing some of those low-hanging fruit ideas and speak deeper on a subject, which will relate your authority and knowledge with your audience.

Brainstorming can be done in a group or by yourself if you're focused and disciplined. However, the most effective brainstorming comes from a diverse set of independently creative and critical thinking peers for whom you have respect. The idea in a brainstorming session is positivity. Just as with improv, say "No" to "No". "No" is off limits on the improv stage. Instead, we say, "Yes! And...". Rather than invalidating and dismissing the previous energy or idea by saying, "No", we say, "No", to "No", and "Yes!" to "Yes! And...". That's not mine. That's standard theatre and improvisation philosophy. Theatre 101.

We apply that into our brainstorming sessions, and we come in with a "there are no bad ideas" mentality. Granted, we all know there are bad ideas. The Shake Weight™ commercial, for example. My philosophy is to take all ideas together as relative equals, mentally flagging some for later reconsideration one way or another, while shelving the – let's say "lower tiered" ideas after the session. It's a way to make everyone feel important, valued, and like they're contributing, which they are. The idea is more to maintain a positive energy which will facilitate more ideas to flourish. Those bad ideas, even if we realize they are not on par, might inspire thought in someone else in the session. What is almost guaranteed is that striking down an idea in front of everyone results in feelings of inadequacy, humiliation, and rejection. It is unlikely this collaborator will feel like their other ideas would be any more valuable. We shut down when those feelings arise. We put our walls up to protect ourselves. And that puts a halt to our creative processes – and the creative processes of others in the brainstorming session as well.

If we are brainstorming ideas by ourselves, and we follow this same tactic, we will be kinder to ourselves in our creative process, fostering less negativity. Remember what I said previously about gaslighting yourself with self-deprecation. Even "Oh, no that idea was stupid" is negative self-talk that can hinder your own process with your solo brainstorming. Remain positive and generous, always looking for the silver lining, even in those "bad ideas". This will encourage outside-the-box and Big Picture First thinking. Big Picture First Thinking is where you take the cliché "step back and see the bigger picture" and flip it. Rather than "stepping back", we see the bigger picture first, training ourselves through information and education, to see a given issue from as broad a view as possible, considering more and more perspectives before "stepping in" to see how that affects you. Stepping back to see the bigger picture puts ourselves at the primary focus and concern, when the issue might not affect us as much as we initially react.

These techniques will help with training your brain for brainstorming. As a content creator or social media personality, it's training and conditioning your mind like one would their body for a marathon. Eventually, you will begin to analyze a topic from more angles and discuss them in ways that everyone else is not.

COLLABORATION

Teamwork makes the team work, right? Finding a community of like-minded, similarly goal-oriented individuals is key to your growth. We need those who can inspire us when we require a recharge and recharging others who fall into their lulls is just as beneficial to us. We are in this together and together, we are stronger.

Some of my closest friends today are those with whom I began to collaborate in some capacity and that mutual creative passion grew a friendship. It is important to build those networks and collaborative relationships with others, especially in your content creative process.

Later in the book, we will discuss more about networking and community building, on a broader scale. For now, look at collaboration as a band. Sure, someone playing the guitar can be entertaining. However, throw a drummer, a bassist, a keyboardist, some horns, maybe a good singer and you have a band. Take away one of those and the sound will not be as cohesive or enjoyable.

When you establish who you are, what you are about, and how you will manifest your goals around that, it is important to be open to other input and opportunities.

As a podcaster and one-man-band content creator, I often find myself overwhelmed by everything I have on my 'To-Do' List. I must write, record, produce, edit, upload, distribute, market, and then write MORE for the online posts. Had I the budget, I would employ talented people to do some of that work – specifically video editing.

It is not self-serving to understand that every relationship is transactional. At the very foundational level, we are exchanging energy. The intent in forming and maintaining a relationship determines selfishness or selflessness. Occasionally, when my schedule permits, I contribute to lower budget projects that sound interesting, because I feel it is my duty to give back to those working to achieve their dreams. Part of this is personal and professional philosophy but it also goes much deeper than that. It isn't hoping karma rewards me, it's understanding that in some way, it all evens out. Or it doesn't. The important thing is the opportunity to learn from an experience and be a part of something.

Collaboration brings out the best in all parties, when done properly. It can also bring about those relationships you will look toward down the road as your respective careers and journeys continue. Being open to collaborative relationships and opportunities while being positive, creative, and generous will bring about the most effective results.

SHOW PREP

Let's discuss the idea of preparation and planning. How often does it seem like someone just turned on their camera and started talking without knowing what they were going to say? In radio broadcasting, regardless of the time of day your program would air, the talent doesn't often walk in without having put some thought into what they'll talk about. If hosting an interview, you would brush up at very least on the basics of whom you are interviewing. Not only is it courtesy, but it also ensures you look prepared and professional.

In broadcasting, specifically radio, it's called Show Prepping. When I hosted morning shows, I would spend the period immediately after the show, while it was still fresh, brainstorming and collaborating with my partners. We would bring ideas to the table, and I produced some show maps breaking down every talking break, printed music logs of all the songs we would play. More music was scheduled than we would be able to play, so we would prioritize the drop-order of the songs, if needed, to ensure we were playing the best of the best mix of songs.

More importantly, we had to make sure we got to our point. In a moment, I will cover consumer attention spans, and something called Word Economy. Often, the talent is not aware or does not care about the audience's desire for "short and to the point". I have coached talent across that spectrum. Those who are unaware will react embarrassed that they are not as polished and sharp with their content, knowing they have work to do. The other end of that is the talent who simply believes the audience will tolerate the rambling, forgiving the sidesteps off topic, because whatever is so appealing to the audience about that talent will outshine the harsh realities of the audience's attention span and on-demand media landscape. It is important to bench the ego when discussing preparation, because feelings aside, the facts speak for themselves. The most successful and popular personalities, regardless of the niche, respect their audience's time and attention. Because of that, often they command that time and attention.

While appointment media consumption is on the decline, consistency is still king. When the audience knows you are offering consistent content that is not only cutting edge, but also concise, they know they can count on you for that goldmine of instant gratification. When the talent talks a lot about nothing in particular, and the audience has to sit around and wait for them to get to the point, it can create a passive following. In this case, imagine your subscriber or follower gets a notification you are livestreaming. It is the difference between them stopping what they are doing to join or thinking, "if I had nothing better to do, I might click, but I don't have time for that right now".

You certainly want to deliver on your audience's expectations consistently. Most audiences today, most people, require brevity, or at least compelling content in lieu of brevity. Sometimes, short and to the point is not possible or does not do the topic being discussed the justice it deserves. However, this philosophy of brevity and less is more is not only about saying more in a shorter period. It is a filter to apply to the content you create. It is a constant evaluation of the content, your take on that content, and how you can convey your take to the audience with respect to their expectations, time, and attention span.

You can achieve this better through proper preparation. As with radio, when I would get into the studio at 5AM with my well-prepared show map in hand, I could hit the ground running, moving things around, if necessary, but always with a plan of action should things go awry. Sometimes, a much bigger story broke between the finalization of the show map and the next morning. Having that show mapped out meant fewer missed opportunities to maximize the airtime.

I encourage you to approach whatever you do as a show, just like any other media outlet. This will help sharpen your preparation and planning of that show, ensuring you are offering an entertaining experience for your audience. Consistently doing that can help your platform and audience grow.

Professional and amateur. Those words have definitions, and usually when we consider those, financial compensation or some level of validation or recognition come to mind. For social media, that certainly can be true. However, professional, and amateur, as I mean it, is in your attitude. Are you a professional? Do you treat your audience, your guests, your content with respect? Do you plan and prepare, analyze the data to see where you can improve, and constantly seek learning and growth?

Or is this something you "just do". You might create content, livestream, or post, but there is no deadline or real consistency. If you decide to livestream, do you plan your guests or just talk to whomever comes in? Is there a topic? Is there a set time to start? To end? Do you look professional doing the content? Do you communicate in a professional manner?

Do not get discouraged. Most on social media fall into the latter more than the former. This is partly because of the financial aspect. Those who are earning from their efforts can afford to take that extra time. They are usually part of a bigger network, too. For the amateur content creator, it is often flying by the seat of your pants. However, nearly every platform allows you to schedule your livestreams, and there are services that will automatically post to multiple platforms simultaneously. There are ways to BE professional, they usually just require an investment. However, those things may be achieved without a budget, it just requires more work on the part of the content creator.

Are you a professional or an amateur?

The trick is understanding your audience. I am a professional. I have been a professional communicator for my adult life. However, I have still fallen into the amateur trap on social media. I have not always planned my livestreams, so my audience cannot always count on knowing when I am live. My various platforms have not always seen the growth that comes with consistency, for a variety of reasons. It is not enough to just create content. Once you do, there is a lot to do to ensure that content is seen and benefits your platform. Again, preparation is key.

Before you turn on a microphone, before you switch on the camera, be sure you are prepared. A little effort up front can ensure your brand has every opportunity for growth possible. Plans can change and it is important to be fluid enough to go with the flow of where the content, topic, or audience takes you, but at very least going in with a default plan will ensure your audience will feel like you are professional, even if you are not.

To that end, it is not always optimal to appear too slick, polished, or professional in some cases. In the social media landscape, the 'realness' of the space is what sets it apart from traditional broadcast media. For many today, suits and ties, hair and makeup, and the high production value of content can turn them off and make them feel out of their league. It can come off trying too hard, among other things. The goal is to make your content look and sound as professional as possible while holding true to the authenticity your audience expects.

Understanding the aesthetics of your content, production quality, preparedness, and some best practices, as you will learn throughout this book, will help. It does not have to be a cable network primetime news channel to be professional. You just must take pride in the final product and take it, your message, your mission, and your audience seriously.

UNDERSTANDING ATTENTION SPANS

A few decades ago, those in media, marketing, and advertising were in a panic because broadcast advertising was going through a shift, thanks to new data. Along with the rise of "commercial free" subscription competition challenging the status quo of consumer attention, data began to suggest that the average attention span of the media consumer was nowhere near what we assumed. The days of sixty second ads were winding down; thus, revenue would be affected. Not only that, to the listener, they count time AND ads. In that, six thirty second ads will sound longer than three one-minute ads.

Today, those attention spans have dwindled to unbelievably low numbers. In fact, just when most in the industry began to wrap their heads around the fact that a sixty second commercial was falling on mostly inattentive ears, tuned-out and turned on to another one of their presets, we saw thirty second ads becoming just as tedious for the consumer. We were finding if we wanted to grab their attention, we had to do it from the very beginning of the message. This is why so many car dealer ads start with some obnoxious sales manager who has no business being in front of a recording device screaming at you.

Get to the point and do it fast. Instant payoff. In a bit, you will learn about the 80/20 Rule and how you can apply that to your content. This is a broadcast news strategy that you are familiar with whether you realize it or not.

Social Media attention spans are different than those of broadcast media. This is because with social media, the consumer has total control over their experience. If they want more cooking videos to show up, they follow more chefs and engage with more food content. Radio and television, broadcast at least, cannot accommodate the consumer that way. That is why streaming services with AI algorithms that learn what you like and offer options individually crafted for the consumer are becoming more viable options for entertainment like music and personality-driven talk radio.

Social Media consumer attention spans, as of the time of this book's release, is around THREE SECONDS. That is one, two, three – and they're gone.

It is ok to bookmark where you are for a moment if you need to take a moment to let that sink in. Within three seconds, five if you are lucky, your audience, on average, has decided whether they will watch another five seconds or so. Then, it is a constant evaluation of interest versus time invested. Have you ever given a video a chance and then decided it was not what you hoped for but you decided to wait it out a few more seconds and then you feel like if you spent all this time watching it you may as well watch until the end?

That is not positive engagement. While your algorithm will benefit and your metrics will shine, the consumer has been left with a negative impression, having watched that much of the video out of a sense of obligation resulting in an expectation unfulfilled.

Our goal, when creating content, is to find the most impactful and meaningful start to the idea and maintaining that momentum throughout the content with a significant enough payoff at the end where the audience will walk away feeling like they want more of what you just delivered. Read that sentence again and realize that I am talking about impactful and meaningful to the audience, not the creator. Knowing your audience will help you deliver content important to your audience.

Three seconds is all you have and that is not easy to accomplish. Understanding is the first step to practicing, which will lead to mastery.

WORD ECONOMY

The idea of The Economy of Words is just that. Word Economy. Go back and read that again. Rather than explaining it "The Economy of Words", it's called "Word Economy" – using two words rather than four. In fact, as you are reading this, I am deliberately overexplaining this as an example of Word Economy.

Word Economy is saying as much as possible in as few words as possible. Word Economy is eliminating pointless words. Word Economy is concise.

Twitter, also known as *X,* did more for Word Economy than any other social media app since Music.ly. When Twitter debuted, you were limited to 140 characters. While that expanded and grew over time, the idea at first was saying the most in the least. Twitter conditioned many to be brilliant but brief. Smart but succinct. Funny in fewer.

Apply Word Economy and Tweet Philosophy to your content. Trim it down and be disciplined in your self-editing. This is not to say you should work tediously to edit out every "umm", "and uhh", etc. I am suggesting, with practice, as you go, be conscious of your audience's limited reading level and attention span. That is not being mean. We all have so much going on, it is natural that we turn to something that does not require us to start, forgive the plug, Overthinking Everything.

Things that can assist you in Word Economy are a deep vocabulary or a simple trip to Thesaurus.com. Typing in a word brings up synonyms, antonyms, definitions, pronunciations, in a matter of clicks. This can aid with repetitiveness and finding alternative words that might be more appealing to your audience or topic.

Short and to the point. That is the direction the media is going. Attention spans aren't likely to improve any time soon. So, without "dumbing it down", aim to keep it simpler. Even with my content, writing, and creative endeavors, I struggle with simplifying my language. This takes practice, but I promise the payoff will be prosperous.

80/20 RULE

The 80/20 Rule is a tried and true, tested strategy of audience retention going back decades. You're probably most familiar with this from broadcast news.

"Coming up, a woman takes out the trash, and you won't believe what she found!"

You've got the 80% of the story you don't need and the 20% you want is held until after you watch their commercials. You get the gist, but you still don't know where this took place or what she found. It's like a joke and you have to wait for the punchline. For a very long time in America, audiences waited. For too long, audiences had no other choice. Social media changed that.

Audiences wait no more. Today's instant gratification society demands those answers now. Failing to provide them in a timely manner, without jumping through the obligatory hoops of non-consensual advertising messages does not build brand loyalty or any favor with those consuming your content. In fact, with whatever information you DO provide them, they will just hit the preferred search engine, type in a few words from that teaser, and negate the need to sit through the commercials.

Have you ever gotten a notification on your phone of a headline from a news story? Those practice a version of the 80/20 Strategy. However, when you click on that story, you are taken to a website that asks you to subscribe to keep reading. Audiences won't have any of that foolishness, so they simply search for keywords and find the story elsewhere, where they have no roadblocks to their satisfaction.

How can you utilize this age-old, yet tired tease without alienating those you are hoping to influence?

Flip it on its ear! For the modern social media audience, part of what will set you apart as a personality is being known for something. In the on-demand world of instant gratification, give them the 20% of vital information in the first few seconds and fine-tune the remaining 80% to be filtered through the perspective only you can offer in your own unique way. The simple fact is that before this culture of entitled instant gratification the gatekeepers of media dictated the terms of the audience's attention span surrender. Today, the audience has the power and the resources to satisfy their need to know and know it now.

Statistics and analytics allow us, as content creators, to see precisely when the audience tunes out of our message. One tactic is to bury yourself in that data to sharpen your delivery, messaging, and strategies. Another tactic is to hold true to yourself, realizing that trying to predict the unpredictable is about as productive as trying to control your audience's habits. The fact is, as I mentioned before in The Ugly Truths, there simply isn't a one-size-fits-all approach to mass communication. This is because the masses are comprised of individuals with their own set of habits, preferences, and quirks. Some of this might be able to be generalized or categorized, but that is why many of the strategies you may discover to grow your online persona are considered "best practices". These aren't the surefire guarantees we all want. They are the best, proven practices.

With the 80/20 Rule, or strategy, you can grab your audience's attention with the vital information they want without "teasing" them with the information they do not consider as important. The word "tease" is what they call this when media personalities use a hook to keep the audience around longer. Who do you know enjoys being teased? In most instances, being teased leaves the target feeling many things, few of them positive. The strongest tactic to audience retention is creating compelling content that makes your audience not just feel but feel positive. Even if the message is a doom and gloom heavy subject like human suffering, the way you deliver the content should not add to the audience's anxiety or emotions consuming the information. That does not mean making light of difficult subjects. Positive does not mean happy or leaving them with a punchline. Positive just means they feel like they want to come back for more – and come back to you for more.

Teasing is also still valuable for audience retention analytics. If you create a three-minute video and you have invested the time and effort into that what good is it if your audience only watches twelve seconds before swiping whichever way for whatever app? So, the 80/20 Strategy becomes the 20/60/20 Strategy.

In a 20/60/20 Strategy, you're leading with the hook of the most vital information but holding something back that is important to the story but will not feel frustrating for your audience to have to wait around for. In between those is most of your content – YOU. You are the difference in the data. How you deliver a message and what you add to that message is what your audience will be tuning in for, however they consume your content. The information is just part of the product. You are the biggest piece of that pie because your unique style and personality will evolve that message into content. That 60% can be opinion, attitude, humor, flavor, etc., but it should be authentic, genuine, and real. It should be YOU.

CRITICALLY THINKING CONTENT

Content creation can seem like an arduous task. In fact, being a content creator can be as frustrating as it can be fulfilling. There will be highs and lows, the blitzes and the lulls. There will be times when the creator will feel the pressure to create with the ideas running dry. There will be periods when things just do not seem to click as easily or naturally and there will be times when the creator has so many ideas, they cannot begin to actualize them all. For a creative individual, leaving an idea on the table can haunt us. That idea almost taunts us. Then, there are those other ideas we hold onto for a rainy day – the day we run out of ideas.

Depending on your niche, organization is key to creating compelling content and growing your brand. Organization, Time Management, Brainstorming, and Mind-Mapping are some ways one can find a rhythm in their creative process. Everyone is different. Find what works for you most consistently. However, again, there are some best practices to consider that might save you a great deal of trouble and time.

In The Compassion and Critical Thinking Workbook, I offered some critical thinking exercises that can help dissect, deconstruct, and reconstruct, for example, a news headline. By looking at that headline in various ways, we open ourselves up to other perspectives and perceptions about that subject. Then, we can reframe the same statement or headline any number of ways to serve any number of agendas.

Critically thinking your own content is fundamental to standing out – setting yourself apart from the personality pack in the constantly cluttered landscape of social media.

Foundationally, this is a philosophy I have embraced since I was on the radio, hosting programs as what many call a disk jockey. If a story breaks, the first few thoughts that come to mind are the same first few thoughts that come into most people's minds when they hear it, too. Do you want to be echoing what your audience has already considered? Possibly, if they seek validation. However, you want to think beyond those first few thoughts and consider just beyond those. Those deeper perspectives are now what some are thinking about in the aftermath of the breaking story – hours or days after. This is still a very strong place from which to create content, so long as you can capitalize on it early. If you give your audience enough time, those thoughts are just as intriguing as that initial low-hanging fruit. Think beyond even those!

Critical thinking is like a marathon. If you try without training you might get a decent way, but at some point, you will sputter out of breath with achy muscles. However, if you are training yourself constantly with peeling back layer after layer of an issue and the opinions your audience might have about the issue, before long, you will not even be considering the first thoughts and the next phase of takes on the issue will seem like the low-hanging fruit. You will have trained yourself to see an issue from any number of different angles, allowing you to be the cutting edge of commentary. Imagine your audience saying "Oh, yeah! I heard my favorite creator talking about that" and "That's interesting. Do you follow my favorite creator? They had the most interesting take I never even considered..."! Both are important. The latter is invaluable word-of-mouth endorsement we, as creators, need.

That is not guaranteed relevance, much less virality, but it will set you apart from the low-hanging fruit of obvious takes. Even the most popular creator offering the obvious takes will become boring to an audience who has already considered that idea.

POSITIVE/NEGATIVE/POSITIVE

In management as well as talent coaching, there is a philosophy of constructive criticism called Positive/Negative/Positive. This means to deliver your message of criticism bookended with positive comments. One could take this approach to content creation, but it only applies in certain niches and scenarios. For example, if the story is about human suffering, leading with a positive and ending with a positive is not always possible or in good taste. However, using that as a filter of consideration is useful. Sometimes, depending on circumstances, that might be effective. However, I want you to think about this from the standpoint of emotional response of the consumer and how they feel consuming your content.

We talked about attention spans and the 80/20 Rule. Now, let's discuss charged molecules. The terms positive and negative are binary and I am just not sure how many things truly are binary anymore. Binary does not leave much room for nuance. However, when it comes to the science of charged molecules, they're either positive or negative, right? Well, not exactly. Some molecules have both a positive and negative charge. Those "Polar" molecules, are attracted to the charges of other polar molecules. You did not come here for a chemistry lesson, so let me skip ahead to the part where this is about creating content.

Positive attracts positive and negative attracts negative. If you have negative content or commentary, don't be surprised when other negative is drawn to you. Same goes with positive. There will always be those trolls who wish only to transfer their trauma onto others. However, if you are creating positive, uplifting content, most of what you draw in should be positive. This idea is not about the message or content we are talking about. This is the feeling of the audience consuming that content.

Furthermore, in the structure of your content, just like the 20/60/20 example before, Positive/Negative/Positive applies a little deeper as well. Examine this from the standpoint of how your audience feels about the content you are creating. It would be easy to list various words for emotional responses and then categorize them into positive or negative, but I'm afraid this is not that simple.

Bad news can still leave your audience feeling positive or negative. It is either a plus or a minus. If you are not catching them early enough with the information they need, you risk losing their attention and eventually their loyalty. Even the bad news can leave a feeling of satisfaction that the need for the information has been achieved. Feeling frustrated, manipulated, or disappointed are negative audience reactions you want to avoid altogether, but especially bookending your content with those. You don't want any of these in the beginning of your content because they won't stay for the rest. You don't want that at the end because that's the impression they are left with. It is ok for the audience to feel frustrated with the facts, events, or story. However, that frustration should be directed at how you, the content creator, is framing or offering it.

Imagine my Bob Barker "help control the pet population" example from before. Not only did Barker use Word Economy, but he also left out the negative part that is important to his cause. If we do not take preventative measures to keep pet animals from breeding, their tendencies can lean more aggressive. That is just the tip of that depressing iceberg. Imagine if Bob Barker closed out The Price is Right every episode with the following:

"Thank you for watching and remember to help control the pet population and have your pets spayed or neutered. If you don't, then millions of dogs and cats will have to be killed, so do your part so we don't have to keep killed cats and dogs."

I do not think it matters how fun The Price is Right was to watch all those years, but I also cannot imagine an audience feeling very good about tuning in tomorrow to hear the same message. That is a very negative statement that does not foster positive, feel-good vibes. Simply asking to support spaying and neutering leaves the dark truth of that mission out. While that truth is valid and the foundation for Barker's cause, expressing that risks tune-out more than building support.

If you are going to leave your audience with negative feelings, carefully craft your content around that and stick it between the positive. This is where your personality can shine. This is why finding your voice and figuring out who you are as a creator is essential to growing your platform and your brand.   Remember to leave your audience with a positive feeling about you as a content creator and the content you create.

BANG! BOOM! POP!

You might be seeing a trifecta trend between 20/60/20, Positive/Negative/Positive and now BANG! BOOM! POP!, but this is a continuation of the same idea. Becoming a social media personality, or any kind of influencer who will affect others, requires great skill and an understanding of entertaining others and entertainment. You do not have to be an entertainer to understand entertaining. Even many entertainers struggle with understanding their own industry sometimes. But bigger is not always better. In fact, in the modern social media age, the more slick and polished content created, the more risk one has of being dismissed in that space.

When someone is scrolling social media, seeing a polished, professional delivery can seem too formal and cold. The social media atmosphere is filled with wanna-be would-be this or that. The audience often follows authenticity. For whatever reason, today that authenticity is illustrated by looking disheveled, sitting on your couch or in your parked vehicle ranting about whatever is on your mind. As unprofessional and amateur as that might appear, it is the genuine and authentic relatability to which many in your audience will cling.

Remaining true to that authenticity while creating content that leaves your audience satisfied and feeling positive about you, the content creator, is a challenge. Now, let's complicate it all by adding showpersonship into it – some pizazz!

As you create content that is eye-catching and attention-grabbing, it is important that the content be structured in a way that delivers attention-retention. Building on the attention span and economy of words ideas a little more and folding in some of our more recent sections of this book, BANG! BOOM! POP! is a strategy to remind yourself, as you structure and create your content, to ask yourself a few questions.

First, does your content start off with a bang, and are you boom, boom, booming through it to end with a pop?

BANG! BOOM! POP! is a philosophy on how to stand out while offering content that's never boring. Start with a Bang! Continue with Booms! End with a Pop!

Plain and simple.

What does that mean? Absolutely nothing, on its own except onomatopoeia. As a filter of content creation, it can be an important coat of lacquer that makes your content shine!

Thinking in terms of a massive fireworks show for example, they start with a huge "BANG!" that gets the audience Oohing and Ahhing. Throughout the middle, there are constant "BOOMS!" that deliver a satisfying buildup for the grand finale of "POP!".

Be that fireworks show and leave your audience mesmerized, telling everyone they know about it, asking, "Hey, did you see THIS?!"

MIC DROP MOMENTS

We all want them, yet they are the white rabbit of social media content – Mic-Drop Moments. Beyond the viral video phenomenon, Mic-Drop Moments leave your audience surprised, enthralled, and waiting for your next drop. If I could teach you how to make a Mic-Drop Moment, I would charge more for this book. That takes a more one-on-one, individualized approach and lots of work to hone that skill.

However, consistently thinking in terms of Mic-Drop Moments and delivering those consistently, will have your audience hanging on the edge of their seats with the "what will they say next" anticipation. If you have ever watched professional wrestling, you know of those Mic-Drop Moments. The promos and trash talking that wrestlers do are written and designed to get the audience excited or feeling a certain way. When the wrestling bad guy, or heel, steps up to the microphone and criticizes the town, the fans, or other wrestlers trying to build "heat" against themselves, it is by design so when they get what they deserve it is all the sweeter for the audience. Justice has been served.

Do not fall into the habit of thinking of this as "punchlines", because when someone tries to be funny and falls flat, the internal response for the audience is awkwardness, uncomfortableness, and negative in most cases. Your Mic-Drop Moments will come from your authenticity, from a place of genuine reaction, and will express your feelings, helping your audience relate to you. This is where planning ahead and all the things you learned in this section come into play. Preparing ahead will help you think about those Mic-Drop Moments ahead of time. Sure, there is nothing like the authentic, improvised, in the moment Mic-Drop Moment, but you must be witty and talented to just come up with those on the fly – and even that takes practice. Sometimes these moments come when we least expect them. Sometimes they come from someone else in your content or livestream. Thinking in terms of "this is good content, but where is the Mic-Drop Moment?" can be a beneficial filter when considering content to share and create. There does not always have to be a Mic Drop Moment. It is better to consider that before posting content than posting your content, then having that lightbulb go off where you think how much better and more effective it would have been had you thought of that Mic Drop Moment sooner. We have all had those moments in real-world conversation, haven't we? Where we walked away thinking, "Dang! I wish I would have said _____".

Train your brain to think in this manner as you create content, and those Mic-Drop Moments will come more naturally.

Section 4:

BRANDING BEYOND SOCIAL MEDIA

The issue with personality branding is that there are a lot of people who need the service, but few resources are affordable and available to most. This section is a simplified version of a much more in-depth one-on-one consultation I offer clients.

In this section, you will learn more about the importance of consistency in your messaging, but also your online identity, personality, content, and quality. You will learn more about taking yourself from a consumer of an app to a content creator on that app to an online brand that transcends one app, to a media personality ready to be noticed by a broader audience.

There is no shortcut to success. There are no blueprints for blowing up. There is no guarantee for growth. There are best practices and standards and those change per platform and with time. You have figured out who you are and what you are about. You have determined why you are doing all this. You have learned some of the philosophy behind the responsibility of mass communication and social influence. You have even learned some tips and tricks of the trade to create more compelling content more consistently. Now, let's discuss how to make all that BIGGER and BETTER!

YOUR ONLINE IDENTITY

We have discussed the journey of self-discovery in who you are as a social media content creator. Now, let's discuss making THAT a brand!

Many in today's social media space are known by a screen name, username, or another witty pseudonym. Most content creators do not use their real names or even a stage name. They are random, quirky, and often confusing. Many times, they are an inside joke, only to the creator themselves. Often, they are unmemorable, unremarkable, and the audience struggles to put the username with the face or content.

RocketMan76 could tell us any number of things about the creator. Apologies if the username is real. I just picked it out of my head as an example. Maybe that person is a fan of Elton John, thanks to his hit "Rocketman". Maybe that person is an actual rocket scientist with a sense of humor. Maybe they were born in 1976, or the account was created when they were 76 years old. Or they might be a misguided nationalist whose every account harkens back to the formation of the United States, 1776. Still, all that aside, what does RocketMan76 tell you about that personality? Nothing specific. Nothing special.

So, what do you hope might be a memorable takeaway from consuming that creator's content? You simply do not know. There is no blanket, one-size-fits-all answer here, but simplified, the idea is choosing an online identity that speaks to who you are, what you offer, and is easy to spell, recognize, and convey to others in any space.

The username "Op3n_M!nd$" does not clearly read as "Open Minds". But, if "Open Minds" was taken, the individual gets creative. However, when introducing himself to others, he has to say, "follow me social media! My username is 'OpenMinds', but it's O, P, the number three, N, underscore, M, exclamation point, N, D, dollar sign." At "the number three", you have lost most people.

The other problem with that kind of online identifier is, while unique and different, there is no real way to market that with a website URL or in any other form of marketing. The more confusing it is to say and spell, the more difficult it is to convey and sell.

Using your own name to brand yourself is not always optimal, as that reduces your anonymity and increases the odds someone might cross appropriate social boundaries. However, while most of us could name a handful of social media monikers, the names of celebrities, infotainment authorities, and other public figures are exponentially longer. Being known **for** something is essential, however it is harder to be known **for** something specific if you are not known **as** something specific.

There is no clear right answer, but there are many wrong directions when considering your online identity and identifier.

Here are some ideas to keep in mind:

- Give yourself 15-20 characters to play with. That is too many but allow some flexibility to ensure you plant your flag on fertile soil, so to speak.
- Avoid things like clever alternate spellings, punctuation, and numbers. Every letter has a sound that is likely two or three letters long, sometimes longer. Those clever spellings might make you chuckle, but they will be much more difficult for your audience to embrace.
- Avoid inside jokes. Again, if it is something you must spend too much time explaining, it is unlikely that you will build much rapport with your audience over that username you came up with and three of your oldest friends found funny. Open to the masses and dig deep to solidify your space.
- Punctuation can be multiple words. Explaining that, verbally, becomes challenging and confusing. Things like "underscore" and "dash", "forward slash, "back slash", and "hashtag" or "pound sign" are things to avoid. These do not always work in every online space and can cause other issues as well, depending on how and where you use them.
- To thine own personality be true but be wise about it. Maybe you like heavy metal, and you decided on Motorhead91. You will

find many racing fans or afficionados of muscle cars might flock to your content before fans of the band Lemmy fronted. Critically think your username and online identifier can help one see the various different ways a moniker can be interpreted. Eggman could be a chicken farmer, someone who really enjoys a good scramble, or someone who is a fan of a certain animated, blue, speedy hedgehog's archenemy. Consider the various ways what you're deciding on could be interpreted.

- IdentifiER, not identifierS. This is a K.I.S.S. philosophy, and we aren't back to rock bands. Keep It Seriously Simple. Without delving into insults on anyone's intelligence, acknowledge the attention span of your audience and respect that most of them will not think as deeply to figure out what you mean as you do. You want A username that you can carry with you across multiple platforms so you do not confuse your audience or ask too much of them by saying, "On TikTok, I am _____ and Insta, Facebook, and Snap, I'm _____. Find me on YouTube as _____". Even your most passionate fans will struggle to find you elsewhere.

YOUR LOGO

If defining your online identity is the next evolution of your social media personality, then solidifying your online identifier is the next step of turning your personality into a brand. Think of every brand out there. They have a few things in common. One of those is a logo.

This is a journey of building legitimacy for yourself in the online, social media space. There are benefits of professional logo design which outweigh the downside of some in your audience feeling like you are "too big for your britches". In fact, a logo allows you to brand and watermark your content, ensuring if anyone shares it or uses it, your brand is front and center. That is not always respected. Like when conservative political mouthpiece Ben Shapiro used one of my videos in his online program where he attempted to roast or mock those with opposing views, he blurred out my logo. While unethical and unprofessional, the removal of such branding is, essentially, stealing in today's social media space.

Branded content, logos, etc., are the calling cards for where an audience might find more about us, if they so choose. Ultimately, it is up to the individual on where they stand on this type of use of content and how they attribute it, but on a positive note, look at it like reaching down to help others get where you are, or where you hope to be. Blocking out, covering up, or cropping out a logo can come off petty, underhanded, and untrustworthy.

Your logo should be clear, eye-catching, and definitive of your brand and message. At first, I had the voiceover cliché of a microphone and waveforms in my logo. The waveform is of me saying "Josh Brandon Voiceovers", which I still incorporate into my current logo. Gone, though, is the microphone, which looked nothing like my actual studio mic, or most microphones used since the 1960's. Instead, a side profile of my face with the brain inside, a maze. That icon, which I use in my Josh Brandon Media logo as well as my similar podcast brand logo, serves as the "O" in Overthinking Everything.

Again, when it comes to logo design, simple is better. Despite my brand, don't overthink it too much. You will want to consider different layouts, dimensions, how it will look and stand out in various sizes, thumbnails, etc. Some go for black and white, others full color. Incorporating something personal, if that makes sense, might be something to consider as well.

It needs to be something that you feel works for you but put some critical thought into it. I saw a logo for a company online that used the "OK" hand-sign with the index finger and thumb forming the O and the three remaining fingers extended, like the actor John Cena used when he wrestled in WWE. While that worked for the company's branding at one point, that hand gesture, having been embraced by white supremacists in recent years, is one of those unfortunate, out-of-our-control factors that might prompt one to reimagine or update their logo and branding.

I could put this to the test and flash dozens of corporate, product, or brand logos in front of you, even with the company name blanked out, and many would score very high.

Logos are iconic, memorable, and definitive of a brand. A great deal of money, time, research, and expertise goes into creating a logo for these brands. You do not have to expend all those resources, but you should consider the importance of logo branding when having yours designed by a friend or on an affordable freelance site.

Think of your logo like you might consider a first tattoo. You will have to live with it for a long time and changing it can be a hassle. So, try your best to make the best decision the first time.

YOUR SOCIAL MEDIA PRESENCE

With your online identity defined, your online identifier narrowed down, and your logo in mind, where will you put that logo? That's your profile picture on all your branded social media accounts. Even if you do not use a specific platform, claim your squatter's rights there, before someone else does.

Selecting a clear and concise online identifier, username, or identity for social media can be trickier than you might think thanks to social media. Because the internet is a vast wasteland of abandoned accounts and dormant identities, you might come up with the most creative and brilliant identifier, only to find out it has already been taken.

Back to the ol' drawing board. In this "Choose Your Online Adventure" book, please turn back to the beginning.

Social media @'s (ats) are today's calling card. We've covered that in the first part of this section. So, if you have that, make sure you have it everywhere. Sign up for a single email account dedicated to that online identifier and then start your accounts with that username, even if you have an already established online persona and accounts on that site.

Even if you are already a brand, you want to secure your branded content as well. If you are on a platform with your real name, start a page for your online persona, wherever you are seeing the most engagement. If your accounts on the other platforms are low engagement, consider changing those names to the new identifier you decided on, if those platforms allow it. If not, reference that the branded account belongs to you with a link to it and include that in your bio on your original platform.

If you are "BarryFanilow" on one platform, secure @BarryFanilow on every platform. I sound repetitive on this point, but it really is that important. Imposters are a real threat to your brand integrity. Poseurs pretending to be you, copying your profile picture and information, adjusting one minor, unnoticeable thing about your username, and sending toxic messages to your followers is a mess you do not want to have to clean up. That is something over which you have little control. You can, however, own the name, own the space, and own the brand everywhere you can.

Once you have your branded username or branded online identifier locked down everywhere, it is vital to your growth as a content creator and on those specific platforms, to formulate a strategy for successful integration of those platforms with the content you create. Again, this is just a sliver of a much larger one-on-one consultation, but it is important that you understand how utilizing each individual platform should be used to grow your brand.

YOUR WEBSITE > a link page

Many on social media will have all their social media accounts and relevant suggested links for their followers on a subscription link stack site. The benefits of this are that the creator has a dedicated short link, while often unbranded, to post in their bios or link to their accounts. That way, when they say, "link in bio", the consumer only needs to click that link to go to another page where they will need to click a bunch of other pages.

Once you become serious about branding yourself as a social media personality, the move away from the amateur link stack to the legitimized website is natural and essential. These things – your branded online identifier, your logo, your socials, your content – are all calling cards to let others know more about you. For a comparable investment to a link stack site subscription, you can have a fully functional legitimate website where you can manage and control the content.

This requires maintenance, which is why many choose the link stack subscription service. However, with today's website technology so user-friendly, you no longer must be an expert in code to build your own site or have one built for you that you then maintain. Having your own branded website is the next phase of development of your brand and a similar philosophy to cyber-squatting on the social platforms you do not use just to have the username on that platform. Your website is the same.

There may be some upfront costs associated with building your own website, but month-to-month hosting versus a link stack subscription site could be comparable in pricing with the advantage being for whatever difference, having your-branded-username-dot-com versus whatever-link-site-you-use-dot-com-slash-maybe-your-branded-username-if-you're-lucky.

www.JoshBrandonMedia.com

www.linkstacksite.com/JoshBrandonMedia

Often, the latter does not look that clean. But, going to that link only offers the consumer more links for them to click and little control for the content creator's customization.

Stand out with a website that not only showcases your personality, your work, your logo, and you, but also legitimizes you, as a content creator and social media personality. For all those products, companies, and brands we thought of off the top of our heads in the section about logos, each one of those has a website. You should, too.

MERCH STORE AND MORE

The ugly truth notwithstanding, my friends, there are possibilities and opportunities to earn in the social media space. Your branded online identifier could lead to merchandise. While not every creator will be able to capitalize on things like mugs, t-shirts, stickers, hoodies, hats, etc., the option is there if that fits your brand and content.

There are services that make it easy to design products and sell them, link them to your socials, in some cases, and create a potential income source. If a catchphrase takes off, or something goes viral, make a product. Be creative on current events and think outside-the-box. If this is within your creative wheelhouse, do not be afraid to take advantage of the opportunity.

Realistically speaking, as I have mentioned many times before, set your expectations low and be surprised rather than feeling disappointed if it underperforms. Your cost, in most cases, is the time it takes to establish the online store, any costs that site might charge for an account, and the time it takes to create your merchandise. It helps to get proof versions or buy your own at cost so you can showcase your merch in your content, so your audience knows it is real, sees it being used, and gets excited about it.

While we create this brand and everything that goes with it in hopes that it might take off, in fact we are creating these things so that we are prepared <u>when</u> something we do takes off. Then, when people search you out, you have everything in place to be taken seriously as a media personality. The audience might like one of your videos, then searches you out and finds out you are much more than just a video, just a creator on an app, and they feel like they are part of something bigger.

Your merchandise should reflect the consumers' wants and needs rather than your own ego. Include shirts that just have your logo, but do not expect those to take off. Instead, place your logo somewhere on your merchandise, but be creative. You could post famous (non-copyrighted) quotes or parodies, jokes, memes, or any number of different ideas that fit your overall brand. The most important thing is to be authentic and original. Stealing someone else's original work is a no-go. So, get creative and create things that, even if they are inspired by another creation, are your original take on it.

Make sure you do your due diligence and know what you can and cannot use in a resale manner for things like – well, anything you might find online, even stock photos. The last thing you want is a cease-and-desist letter and someone wanting to be paid for something you used. Still, having an online merch store means always having something to promote and talk about as a means of tangible support. When your followers buy from you, they are supporting you. They could send you money directly, like a donation. While that might work for some, most cannot count on that happening regularly. The idea of patrons for our art works is different than in ye olde days.

A merch store is a way of increasing the likelihood of your loyal followers contributing to your success while getting something physical and useful in return for their investment in you, as a brand.

A warning to take note of: Taxes and other business obligations may apply. Due diligence, again, will help ensure you do this the right way. Find out what your state or area's specific tax guidelines for online sales would be and prioritize that. Pay your taxes as you go so you are not left with a hefty tax bill at the end of the year.

Section 5:

GROWING YOUR BRAND

To grow your brand, in the social media personality and influencer space, is to become more than you imagined, bigger than you are, and larger than life. Few of us are as interesting as we seem to others. Hopefully, in this journey, you have learned some more of what it takes to make the content you create more interesting and appealing to a broader audience.

Like an animal in a nature documentary, flaring themselves out to seem more imposing to potential threats, an effective strategy for growth is to fake it until you make it – while maintaining authenticity. For the online personality or social media influencer, the approach is like reality television. The reality show personalities are there because they are already larger than life. However, most of them are dialed-up, but dialed-in caricatures of their true, authentic selves. Now that you understand a bit more about how to achieve some of this, let's look at growing your brand beyond a username.

ONE-DIMENSIONAL TALENT DELIVERS ONE-DIMENSIONAL RESULTS

The COVID-19 Pandemic of 2020 showed us many things, but as far as this book and what I hope you take away from it goes, when we were all quarantined and cooped up, locked down and losing our collective minds, we had to get creative and find ways to entertain ourselves. Many found the social media space to be one where more and more people were finding their voice and platforming their unique personality. Perhaps no other event in recent memory facilitated the growth of social media and some content creators/influencers than the COVID-19 Pandemic.

As social media use spiked during this time, downloads of some social media apps peaked as well. Use of specific social media apps, like TikTok for example, grew exponentially in different demographics. While traditionally an app for the younger generation, many in the 30+ age range began using the app and its algorithms to generate a generous following relatively easier than most other platforms. As the events of 2020 unfolded, both health and social concerns began hitting a fever pitch in America and TikTok, YouTube, Twitch, Twitter, Instagram, and Facebook became home to more and more social discourse.

TikTok and the platform's interface, algorithms, and community-building characteristics brought together those who desired a platform to speak their truths and those who wanted to hear it. Content creators and content consumers. While most other platforms' methodologies were more restrictive and difficult to break through for the creator, TikTok's atmosphere, while toxic and problematic, has become ideal to grow at least a moderate following with less effort than its competitors.

Content creators and content consumers – a symbiotic and codependent relationship! The creator needs consumers and the consumer needs content to be created. Without one or the other, the formula does not work. Social media thrives on being the new frontier for personality branding. No longer do you need a degree or an FCC license to broadcast. The gatekeepers are gone. However, social media also thrives on exploitation and what amounts to slave labor.

The content creator, anyone who creates any content for any social media app, platform, or website, often creates this content without being financially compensated. That content is then used, free-of-charge, to promote the app, and generate more money for that platform, often without consideration of the content creator. Even when compensation is offered, it is such a meager percentage of the pie, it is insignificant for most. Many amateur social media personalities might think it's novel to earn a few dollars here and there, without realizing they are offering their time, talents, image, ideas, and personality to provide free content to a platform with pennies on the dollar in return. That's ok, for many, because we do not do what we do for riches, or we would do something else.

Hoping to earn a living, or even side money, from your efforts online comes down to a few things. First, you need to be incredibly talented. Next, you should be diverse in that talent. As discussed earlier, between creating content, broadening your brand, supplementing your skills, perfecting your personality, and delivering on your dreams, it can seem overwhelming, time consuming, and all-encompassing. It is. That is why finding paths to earning amid all that will help keep your brand growing.

Most content creators are not independently wealthy, backed by angel investors, or supported regularly with fan donations. Many are hardworking people who use social media as a hobby, a mission, or in hopes of becoming more. I urge you to dig deep into your dreams and cull your creativity to broaden your brand's impact and potential. Part of that is giving yourself permission – to think outside the box, to be bold, to dismiss criticism while embracing critique – to outperform your potential.

Just as with social media, it has never been easier to accomplish any number of goals, dreams, or creative endeavors. If you want to sing, sing. If you want to write a book, write a book. If you want to host lectures, host lectures. If you want to promote your hobby, promote your hobby. Look at yourself as more than just a username – an account on an app – a content creator. Imagine the things you could be capable of if you just had the time, knowledge, and confidence to do it. Then, do what you only imagined before.

Chances are, you never thought you would be a social media personality or influencer either. Chances are, you have already accomplished things you never thought possible at one point. Whether you have seventeen followers, 17,000, or 1.7 million, it is unlikely your potential has been fully maximized. Make a list of the goals you never thought you would accomplish and the dreams you were scared to admit were true. From that, you might have a clearer picture of the other paths to growth for yourself as a person, as a brand, and as a talent.

When you create, have a strategy for success mapped out on how that content will live and grow in the short and long term. Many content creators create content, post it, and start thinking about the next piece of content. It is vital to keep your creativity flowing consistently, but also reflecting on what you have already created to find ways to make that content live on in the algorithm is also an important strategy in growing yourself and your brand.

For this, let's discuss the RVM Method. Objects in the Rear View Mirror May Appear Closer Than They Are. Once you create something, make it seem much bigger than it is. That means committing to cross posting your content on other platforms, to draw awareness of your brand elsewhere. Once a piece of content exists, formulate numerous ways to promote that one piece of content across the spectrum of your social reach. You can create content in mass quantity, and saturate your social media with videos, posts, etc., or you can create less content, post more on the content you do create, or perhaps adopt a philosophy that is a hybrid of both or other methods. Whatever you decide, RVM! Rear View Mirror. Do not post and look straight ahead to the next thing until you are sure you have maximized what you have already created.

Keep creating. Keep posting. But remember to RVM! Look in your Rear View Mirror and make those posts appear bigger than they were.

Remember that a one-dimensional talent will often yield one-dimensional results. If a content creator wishes to be more than a username on an app, it requires a lot of work. Try new things, expand your horizons, adjust your expectations, and do not be afraid of failure.

Do **not** be afraid to dream!

NETWORKING AND COMMUNITY BUILDING

Among the best strategies for personal growth is building mutually beneficial relationships with fellow creators in your community. Networking with others through other social media platforms and groups can help bring more people to your cause and open you up to more than just your own.

These relationships can offer loyalty and understanding in a space that is not always known for its positivity. In the podcast space, joining online communities of fellow podcasters can help grow a brand by showcasing your skills and accomplishments in front of others who might have suggestions, ideas, or philosophies you hadn't considered. Building a network and community will help you not feel as isolated and 'on your own' in the tedious space of content creation and social media influence. It can also build and grow your brand by offering more platforms for you to guest on, podcasts for example, which would allow you to promote what you do.

More than building within your existing network and communities, assess where you want to go with your career as a media personality/content creator and begin to expand your network to include those niches as well. Do not be afraid to ask for help. Good help rarely comes free these days, but remember you always have something to offer. That is why you are valuable in this space. When building relationships, networking, and gathering a community of like-minded people driven by similar values, consider a barter type system of what you can bring to the table for someone and what you might need as well to help you all grow together.

Fostering and building mutually beneficial and collaborative relationships and friendships will pay off with better content, broader perspectives, and fresher ideas to feed your creativity.

SUPPORT YOUR COMMUNITY AND BEYOND

The major principle to take away from networking and building relationships is to not take more than you give. At least give as much as you take. When you build those relationships, be aware of the support others show you and try to prioritize your support for your community. Be deliberate in your interaction and engagement with other creators. Set your notifications to alert you when they post so, even if you do not have time to consume content regularly, you can at least "Like, Share, and Subscribe". Boosting the content of others in your space will help grow your account and your community. There are added perks of sharing followers, fanbases, and resources as well.

In everything you do, be authentic and altruistic. Your desire and drive to grow and be more can coexist with your values and integrity. You can simultaneously see the value in someone and what they can offer you while genuinely appreciating what you can offer them. Collaborative relationships and community building require mutually beneficial and often transactional interactions and exchanges.

In the past, pioneers ventured out on the wild frontier, ready to confront any challenge head on, but also ready to settle and build, and become self-reliant, as individuals and as a community. The idea is similar in the wild, unsettled frontier of social media. You are on the wagon train with builders, farmers, cooks, teachers, and everything one might need to start a town from scratch and build that community. Identify your strengths and weaknesses, where you thrive and where you struggle. Then, strive to build relationships with those who can fill in some of those blanks for your own journey, and those for whom you can assist in theirs. Not only will your perspective and potential benefit from this, so long as you are doing it for the right reasons, but the bigger that community of mutually beneficial support you build grows, the more guaranteed engagement you should see on your content. In most algorithms, immediate views and engagement determine a lot about that content's success.

The most important thing is do not expect others to support you, your content, or your dreams unless you are willing to at least do the bare minimum in that space for others. It can be hard, as you grow your brand, to remember the many people, creators, and missions you want to amplify with your voice and platform. However, remaining true to those who helped you grow and reaching back to help others grow is essential to us all. We are all stronger together and together we can make a difference. Hopefully, after this book, you will help make a positive difference.

Section 6:

THE ENDGAME

Thank you again for taking the time to read this book. I believe it is lost on many in the era of instant gratification just how important responsibility, integrity, and critical thinking is to not only creating content but being a content creator. Whether your goal, or endgame, is to be a celebrity, an authority, or just find a community to be a part of in the social media space, the information in this book can help you be a better version of yourself in that online space and help make the space itself better.

Identifying your persona and mission, allowing yourself permission to dream big, building and contributing to a larger community to help pursue those dreams, and consistently creating compelling content to help you manifest those dreams into attainable goals and then, into reality are all ideas I have covered in this journey. The final section of this book will cover identifying your goals, ensuring they are realistic and attainable, acknowledging your dreams, regardless of how big they may seem, creating an actionable plan to realize those dreams, and the idea of leaving a legacy with the work you are doing.

IDENTIFYING AND SETTING REALISTIC, ATTAINABLE GOALS

The social media influencer space is saturated with any number of different personality types with various motivations for trying to build a following online. Their goals could be anything from passing the time to passive earning, income, or influence, affecting change, or contributing to the clutter. Determining and clarifying your goals is the difference between your social media career becoming a meandering road trip with little direction, where you are just along for the ride until it ends and mapping out a prepared and deliberate journey. Preparation, planning, and proactivity decides who is in the driver's seat. There is no rule book on goal setting. I suggest you keep it real, and you make it realistic.

The importance of dreaming big cannot be understated. Those big dreams will fuel you in the dark times. However, setting realistic expectations for your online brand's performance is healthier. Have your dream goals – your long-term goals – but also set attainable benchmarks along the way, that are challenging but doable. The risk of setting an unrealistic goal too early is that putting yourself under that much pressure to reach something you may not be ready for can be discouraging, overwhelming, and can psyche you out before you even start.

In my acting career, had I set a goal of being the lead in an established franchise, I would have been disappointed, and every step of the last decade would have been a failure for me. Instead, I have prepared myself internally to be ready if that door ever gets knocked on, but my more realistic goals are still impressive benchmarks to have hit. I obtained talent representation. I got back on-stage doing theatre after 20 years. I got TV roles, film roles, commercials. My voiceover career has brought me various roles including playing a vehicle-morphing robot, a cowled nocturnal crusader who dons a cape and many other roles and projects for leading brands across the globe. All those accomplishments I am incredibly proud of, but had I set unrealistic goals that were harder to reach, I surely would not feel like I achieved as much as I have.

I can still acknowledge my experience, talent, and hard work could and should make those unrealistic goals attainable, while also understanding that, given circumstances beyond my control, the odds are against me. It does not stop me from dreaming, working toward that dream, or being prepared to grab for that ring, should the carousel get me within reach of it one last time. My mental health is better served by hitting realistic benchmarks that leave me feeling accomplished and able to bask in the achievement rather than getting down and questioning myself for not having starred in that blockbuster already.

Your goals, dreams, benchmarks and how you prioritize them are unique to you. Do not be afraid to set the big goals, but do not let those goals hinder you if they do not come to fruition. Keep working and good things will come.

ACKNOWLEDGING YOUR DREAMS

Quite possibly the most difficult part of a journey is admitting to yourself that you have dreams – then acknowledging you want to achieve them. For the troubled soul forged in the fires of trauma, this can especially be true. Self-doubt, low self-worth, confidence issues, and the everyday gaslighting we endure from countless outside influences dictate more of our reached potential than our own talent, drive, and will-to-succeed.

Too often, life gets in the way of dreaming big and it becomes easier and easier to settle for that realistic and attainable goal. As I mentioned, it is important to set those goals because they are huge boosts when you clear that hurdle. However, those are your benchmarks, not the endgame. Your dreams are your dreams, and you are entitled to dream those dreams. You do not have to allow yourself or anyone else to convince you those dreams are invalid or unreachable.

In sales, as I have mentioned before, setting an unrealistic goal may set you up for failure. This is where goals and dreams differ. Your goals are your benchmarks. Your dreams are what you are working toward. Your goal is to score points. Your goal is to win games. Your goal is to win the championship. Your DREAM is to build a dynasty. Now, take that sports analogy and apply that to yourself. What is the dynasty you will build? What is the record you will break? What is the Cinderella story you want to have told for generations to come? None of that is possible without the goals, wins, and championships. Name a dynasty built around losses.

Setting a realistic and attainable game plan for your goals is vital to pursuing your dreams. Today, nothing is out of reach. Success, especially in the social media space, does not come with a blueprint. There are things you can do, strategies you can implement, books you can read, and consultants you can pay to help you grow and improve your content, performance, and brand, but there is no secret anyone can give you that will just unlock the treasure chest of social media relevance, popularity, and virality. In fact, I might argue that if this is what you are looking for, it might be that you are not ready for that responsibility.

The dream must come with some level of altruism and humility. You must be doing this for a purpose larger than your own fame and fortune. In fact, I am not even sure fame or fortune should even be included on the list of "why" one is pursuing a life on social media. It is often intrusive, thankless, and stressful to put yourself out there, day after day, post after post, dealing with the hate, vitriol, trolls, and haters. There is no dollar amount one can place on their mental health and the toll social media takes on the consumer is great. Greater is the toll on the content creator.

Acknowledging your dreams, the lofty ones, the ones that you are afraid to admit to yourself, much less others, is important. Not only will that acknowledgement give you a clearer picture of where you want to go, it will set up your road trip with a GPS and you in the driver's seat rather than flying by the seat of your pants, winging it, relying on road signs to get where you are going with your audience in the driver's seat – if you are lucky.

Give yourself permission to believe. Day in and day out, we choose to exhibit faith in any number of things. Faith in a higher power to faith that traffic light will eventually change. Faith is a funny thing, in fact. We can have faith so easily in so many ways in so many different things. However, finding the faith for our futures – faith in ourselves – seems to be where many fall short. Do not be afraid to have faith in yourself. That will be your strongest ally in any journey of self-actualization you pursue.

Refine your dreams, goals, and the steps it takes to achieve these. Never be afraid to reevaluate what it is you want for yourself. Just be honest, be true to yourself, and never settle for less. Do not give in to gaslighting and watch out for the "whuddabouts". Those "well, what about THIS", which are just safety measures your insecurities use to keep you in check, so you do not get hurt, disappointed, or crushed when those dreams fail to fall into fruition.

Most people who dream of starring in movies never get that big break. Most people who dream of releasing an album never record a single song. Most people who say, "I should write a book", never finish, even if they start. Today, it has never been easier to accomplish any of these things and more – whatever your dreams might include.

There will always be roadblocks, bumps in the road, and immovable objects hindering your journey. Be that irresistible force — a battering ram through the immovable object of brutal reality. Be realistic but dream big. Sounds contradictory, right? So much in today's social media space is. That is why acknowledging your dreams, your goals, and your greater purpose is important. The social media space is one where true authenticity can seem manufactured, if one can find it at all. Avoid being one of the many creators on social media, just doing whatever it takes to grab a following and shine in their 15-minutes of fame. Establish a foundation for long-lasting relevance beyond a specific app, platform, and beyond social media itself.

CREATING AN ACTIONABLE PLAN

Part of any journey, like any road trip, is mapping out the destination, where you will stop to recharge. Fuel stops for your vehicle. Food and rest for your body. These are important, because if your journey is long and arduous, you might risk distracted driving or falling asleep at the wheel. The journey to your dreams is no different.

Creating a plan is only part of the success strategy. Creating an <u>actionable</u> plan with attainable goals and benchmarks makes things easier for you in the long run. While taking a road trip, knowing it takes 18 hours to get where you are going, one might be tempted to risk driving straight through. However, it might be wiser to split that trip up into segments, knowing your vehicle will need fuel along the way and you will, too.

Sometimes, we can mistake our stubbornness for determination. Nothing says you must push on when you feel like you should take a break. Just as I discussed earlier talking about mental health and the overwhelming nature of content creation, it is important to remember self-care in this process. Self-care should be as much a part of your plan for success as anything else. I might argue that without a strategy for self-care, the resulting struggles will hinder your personal and professional growth.

Creating long-term and short-term goals, establishing your destination, acknowledging your dreams, and seeing yourself as a true professional in an amateur space are also very important. Remember, seeing yourself as a professional does not mean dressing up like a major network media celebrity or even the slick production quality of your content. Seeing yourself as a professional is an internal philosophy – a filter – through which you process every decision, action, and idea. Being a professional is holding to standards, ethics, and respecting the responsibility that comes with having a social media megaphone at your disposal.

Being a professional is also preparing ahead with a plan of action to reach your destination that is both realistic and actionable. Your dreams may be lofty. Your expectations should be realistic. Your plan to reach those should be actionable.

Creating an actionable plan is creating a plan for which you can take action to realize that plan. It does not make sense to make a plan that is unattainable by reasonable standards given your resources and realities. If you do not have the financial resources to achieve a goal, your plan-of-action should acknowledge that and offer solutions, workarounds, or some compromise so that your plan is not stalled before you begin – or worse, when you are already in progress.

For example, if your goal is to obtain talent representation, as was my goal several years ago when I officially launched Josh Brandon Media, then there are actionable steps you can take to achieve that goal. The unrealistic plan sets that goal with no real direction to get there or possibly little understanding of the details. You simply know you want an agent, but perhaps you do not understand quite what it is an agent does, how one goes about setting up meetings with agents, or even negotiating contracts once that meeting takes place. The work it takes to put yourself in a position where a talent agent might look at you as a potential earner for their roster is not always considered. However, an actionable plan takes all that into consideration and places you right in the middle of it all. Rather than "email agencies and ask how to get an agent", your actionable plan includes building a resume of work, with samples of that work, and a pitch that clearly showcases what you have to offer that agency so that when that meeting takes place, you walk out with a contract instead of a checklist of things you need to do before contacting them again in 6 months to a year.

Remaining realistic while maintaining positivity and hope can be daunting. However, only through careful consideration of the very real roadblocks we might face will ensure we are prepared should those roadblocks manifest. The actionable plan takes steps to get where one is going. The unrealistic plan is an abstract mission statement that goes nowhere fast and relies on luck.

LEAVING A LEGACY

When I started my journey, I saw the world around me changing and some alarming realities came to light. I was disappointed by so many people as American culture shifted in a direction I always assumed was a social outlier. Then, as more and more normalized abnormalities began bubbling to the surface of society, I could no longer remain publicly silent, privately outspoken. I became more and more publicly loud and proud. However, one lingering thought plagued me and drove me more toward the content I would create surrounding my Overthinking Everything brand.

"If my father was alive today, I wonder where he would stand."

My father was a toxic and problematic man with many undesirable attitudes toward a lot of people. He was a good dad, who sacrificed and provided for me. He was also abusive at times, physically, verbally, and mentally. My dad was funny to many people, but often showed little regard for the targets of his humor. My father was a complicated, yet simultaneously simple man. Still, my hope was that age and granddaughters might have softened his stances on social issues. However, my father died in 2007, before America elected its first black president. I never even got to see how he would have reacted to that event. He left me with so many unhealthy ideas and attitudes, it is hard for me to imagine a dramatic shift in his views.

I did not want that uncertainty lingering over my children. I wanted to be sure my daughters, my family, my friends, and anyone who might stumble across me, on social media, would know where I stood. I wanted no question for my children when issues like humanity, compassion, and ethics were involved. I wanted to make sure my children and their children, my descendants if ever I were to have any, would know where Josh Brandon stood on whatever issue they might question. That led me to my legacy.

What did I want to leave behind?

Then, I began mapping out my journey. Part of that was not saying "No" to myself. I had to stop letting me talk myself out of doing something. I had to begin actualizing my ideas and turning my creations into reality. I wanted to do my own show, so I started Overthinking Everything. I wanted to write, record, and produce music, so I became "Sir TalksALot". I wanted to write books, so I wrote books. I wanted to be in movies and television, so I took the steps necessary to achieve those goals.

The legacy I leave behind will be one where my children will have someone to look up to who did whatever he set his mind to. Hopefully, that will give my children permission to be bold enough to take risks.

On social media, the legacy I wanted to leave was mostly just for myself and anyone who might read my status updates. When I started posting videos, I was doing it mostly for me, for my own sanity, because holding it in much longer was driving me mad. But the underlying legacy in mind was that my children would never have the doubts and questions in their minds that I had about my own father. When the important things happened and social change was afoot, I want them to know I was and would have been right on the front lines of that change rather than standing on the sidelines making excuses as to why I was not ready or willing to accept it.

The lasting legacy I wanted for myself was one of helping others – empowering them to take the leaps of faith I've been able to take in life. I want to inspire others to follow their dreams, which is where My Podcast Workshop comes in. I want part of my legacy to be the podcasts I help others start and the many who are touched and inspired be each of those. That's a ripple effect legacy I could be proud of.

Your legacy is your design and definition. Your goals will lead you closer to your dreams, but so much of that is out of your control and you should not hold yourself accountable for what you cannot control. Do everything within your power to be the irresistible force against the immovable object. Sometimes, even that is not enough. Be forgiving of yourself. Set the rules for your legacy and hold true to those.

Your goals are your benchmarks to refuel and recharge you on the way to your dreams. However, the dreams may or may not come to pass. Your legacy – what you leave behind – will be independent from whether you ever filled in the blank with whatever your dream was.

Start living your legacy now. Do not wait for your dreams to be fulfilled before your legacy begins. Remember, the legacy is the dynasty. That dynasty is built on championships, wins, and points scored. So, go out there, score your points, notch those wins, and bring home some championships. Your legacy begins with the training, preparation, and planning you put into all that.

What do you want to leave behind?

CONCLUSION

I hope this book and the information, advice, and wisdom I have included have helped you. I hope you take advantage of some of what I have learned, through trial and error. I have amassed large followings and lost those followings. I have survived account bans, and suspensions, and the frustration that comes with all that. So much of social media is rejection, vitriol, and toxicity. Even if you are not in a controversial niche, the negativity for negativity's sake can be overwhelming. I encourage therapy, mental health proactivity, a strong inner circle of support and reflective meditation to get through the hard times.

Whatever your niche, whatever your dreams, whatever your journey to get there, remember to always be positive toward yourself, never give up, and keep posting.

Thank you for your support!

There's more to learn about social media and podcasting! I want to invite you to explore the possibilities of podcasting though My Podcast Workshop – a podcasting workshop that focuses on the most important aspect of podcasting – YOU!

Please visit the website to learn more.

Do more than *just* **Create...**

INFLUENCE!

Do not forget that there are additional materials available to help you along your journey and even more related materials, updates, and more on my website at:

www.MyPodcastWorkshop.com/InfluenceBonus

About The Author

Josh Brandon, Host of Overthinking Everything, Voice Actor, Social Media Influencer, Entertainer

Host of *Overthinking*

Everything and author of *The Compassion and Critical Thinking Workbook*, **Josh Brandon** is a career entertainer with experience in television, radio, theatre, and social media. Josh has learned through trial and error, along with grit and  determination, the harsh realities of creating content on social media platforms uses his vast and diverse experience to transform the lives of others through empowering their voices in the podcasting space.

A talent coach with media personality experience spanning three decades, Josh brings his diverse knowledge to social media content creators seeking to grow their brand beyond a single platformas Founder of My Podcast Workshop. For more information on Josh Brandon, please visit:

Made in the USA
Columbia, SC
24 September 2024